The Changing F

Manchester

A fascinating insight into the changing landscape of
Manchester and the surrounding area over the last 150 years

VOLUME 3

at heart 💛 publications

First published in 2007 by
At Heart Publications
32 Stamford Street, Altrincham, Cheshire, WA14 1EY
in conjunction with
Manchester Evening News
1 Scott Place, Hardman Street, Manchester, M3 3RN

ISBN 978-1-84547-160-6

Printed by Bell & Bain, Scotland

Contents

free internet access . family history . talking books .
business information . talks . art . homework centres .
language courses . theatre . help for inventors . DVDs
. free events for kids . festivals . silver surfer clubs .
local images collection . bestsellers . author visits .
CDs . free computing courses . newspapers . mobiles
. community information . brilliant books . displays .
on-line learning . reading groups . CD-ROMs . culture
. local history . books for babies . exhibitions . advice
. workshops . live poetry . sheet music . what's on .
treasures . coffee . videos . storytimes . fun

When did you last visit your library?

www.manchester.gov.uk/libraries

Manchester Libraries & information Service

MANCHESTER
CITY COUNCIL

Manchester city centre and its suburbs continue to evolve over the decades.

Victoria Buildings "Then" and "Now".

It is difficult to believe that Manchester and its suburbs were once rural idylls. Long before the days of cotton and industrialisation the area was filled with farms and small cottage weaving industries. The bustling streets of suburbs like Northenden and Cheadle were once free of heavy traffic, and a horse and cart was the main mode of transportation.

Times change and Manchester became one of the world's leading powers – the birthplace of the Industrial Revolution. The old Tudor manor houses of the city centre were demolished to make way for giant red-brick mills which dominated the skyline. Whole communities sprang up around the mills as industry and commerce became the driving force of the Age.

Today Manchester continues to thrive – gone are the giants of cotton, and in their places are newly refurbished office suites and apartment complexes, as the city continues its transformation into a dynamic world-class metropolis. The city is proud of its industrial past and today's skyline reflects the embracing nature of the preservation of our remaining buildings alongside their sleek glass and steel counterparts.

The third volume in our 'Changing Face of Manchester' series shows the continuing development of the city and its suburbs. From the elegant Victorian and Edwardian street scenes in which trams lined the roads, to our modern bustle where Manchester's Metro service has seen the return of the tram system to the city.

Using the combined photographic archives of the Manchester Evening News and the city's Central Library, we have once more gathered a unique collection of images chronicling the development of the area as it was 'Then', and as it is 'Now'.

In this volume we pay tribute to some of Manchester's historical businesses, many still family-run, whose legacy in the area reach over the decades. Some of the companies like Joseph Holt's Brewery have been instrumental in the commerce of the city and have retained their strong links to the local community. As is the nature of this city, some of the newer businesses have already become part of the rich tapestry of Manchester's history by ensuring the continued use of some of the most iconic architectural landmarks in the area.

We hope you enjoy this glimpse into the changing face of Manchester.

Heaton Chapel Tollhouse

Toll roads were once a familiar aspect of travel in the Manchester area, with turnpikes and toll-houses constructed at points along the road, allowing for fees to be levied at drivers for the use of that stretch of road.

It was a system also designed to maintain the condition of the highways, although many roads did not always seem to see the benefits of improvements. The Manchester to Buxton turnpike was opened in 1725, running along the A6 through Stockport and by the tollhouse featured in our photograph from the 1800s.

The tollhouse, to the left of the open-top tramcar, is at the junction of Wellington Road North and the A626 Manchester Road in Heaton Chapel. The tollhouse at Heaton Chapel served for some years as a branch of the District Bank.

To the right of the photograph is St. Thomas Church and Primary School. The church was consecrated in 1765 but records show that there was a church building on the site in 1758. St. Thomas's church owes its origin, not to one rich landowner as was the norm, but to a group of local contributors, who paid subscriptions for their church pews. This subscription meant that no one, other than the person renting the pew, could use the seating.

The first school building was erected on a strip of land next to the church. The land, donated by Lord Egerton in 1866, was given on the condition that it be used as a school or would revert back to his or his heirs' ownership.

Today the A6 is one of the busiest roads in the area with a steady stream of buses, cars and bicycles going between Manchester and Stockport.

Court Leet at the Red Lion

The name Withington originates from Saxon times, a derivative of 'Withy-ton', meaning 'settlement in a marshy area where willows grow'.

For several centuries Withington remained a rural hamlet, as can still be seen in our mid-1800s image of the popular 17th-century Red Lion public house on Wilmslow Road.

The Red Lion pub has had a long history of serving ale and being a focal point for local people. The building has served as the meeting point for Withington's court leet.

A court leet was presided over by the 'lord of the manor' in order to maintain control and pass judgements on local issues. The court judged everything from the transfer of land, to nuisance neighbours who did not

maintain their lands properly and let their pathways become blocked.

The area behind the pub opens up into a garden and bowling green, and over the years the green has been used to host Inter County Bowling Championships. Indeed, the Red Lion was one of the venues for the first championships in 1907, as Lancashire and Cheshire used the green for their home venue against Staffordshire.

In our older image there is a large sign for the Withington Rifle Range on the side of the building. During the 1860s several Rifle Volunteer Corps were raised in the Manchester area and rifle ranges, as advertised on the side of the Red Lion, offered both locals and Volunteers an opportunity to practice.

Today, Withington is a thriving suburb of Manchester and the image of the area as a rural hamlet is long gone. Withington has a busy shopping area and is home to a thriving student community, that takes advantage of the easy travel links into the city centre.

Tollgate at the Woolpack Hotel

During the 1800s Pendleton experienced, as did many of the other towns surrounding Manchester, an industrial boom reflected in the mills and collieries that were built in the area.

By 1856 Pendleton had built the Mechanics Institute, which would later become part of Salford Technical Institute, and in 1868 the town constructed its own Town Hall.

Our view of the tollgate on Eccles Old Road, Pendleton, is thought to date from around the late 1860s. The Woolpack Hotel, pictured on the right, shows a couple of the hotel's female staff standing outside the door watching the photographer.

Tollgates seemed to be an ideal place to build a refreshment point, which is why many of the pubs like the Woolpack Hotel set-up

their businesses in these locations. However, changing fortunes in the area meant that the hotel finally closed in 1966 after being in business for over 100 years.

The owner of the Pendleton tollgates, John Greenwood, recognised the potential in providing transportation into Manchester city centre. In 1824 Greenwood began a horse bus service three times a day to Market Street in 1824. Most of the passengers using this service seemed to be merchants needing to trade in the city or more wealthy customers who were spending their monies in the thriving shopping district.

Passengers had to pay a fare of six-pence and could be picked up or set down anywhere along the route, similar to the service offered by Manchester's bus companies today.

Today, Pendleton is continuing to thrive as one of Salford's busiest shopping districts and the central point for Salford's bus station allowing workers and students to travel between Salford and Manchester.

The Lost Gem of Smithy Door

During the 16th Century Manchester really began to develop and prosper as a market town.

Industry in the area was continuing to grow and the city was becoming famous for its cotton and textile production. The quality of the cloth was determined by the Court Leet, which standardised the weights and consistency of the textiles.

Many merchants and landowners saw a dramatic increase in their fortunes during the beginning of Manchester's textile boom. One of the notable local men who prospered during this time was Nichols Mosley, who built Hough End Hall in Charlton-cum-Hardy and finally became Lord Mayor of London in 1599.

Trade in Manchester continued to flourish and continual improvements in cloth manufacturing and transportation meant that the city could export its wares all across the UK and even into parts of Europe. Although the expansion of trade brought prosperity to the city it also meant that there was an increase in disease as the city experienced several outbreaks of plague.

Taken in 1865, our image shows one of the lost gems of Manchester – the ornate 16th-century town house of the Sydall family in Smithy Door. This beautiful town house had originally been close to the market place but was finally demolished to make way for the Victoria Buildings and specifically the Victoria Hotel on this site.

When this picture was taken part of the Sydall's house was being used as a pub, the Vintner's Arms, and another part occupied by J Eastwood, an egg, fish and butter merchant. Smithy Door was a narrow winding thoroughfare, once the principal area of Manchester where prosperous merchants and family's chose to live.

Today there is little left to see of 16th-century Manchester as the city has undergone many redevelopments over the centuries.

These develpoments have attracted numerous retail outlets, including Harvey Nichols which now occupies the site of the former Tudor town house.

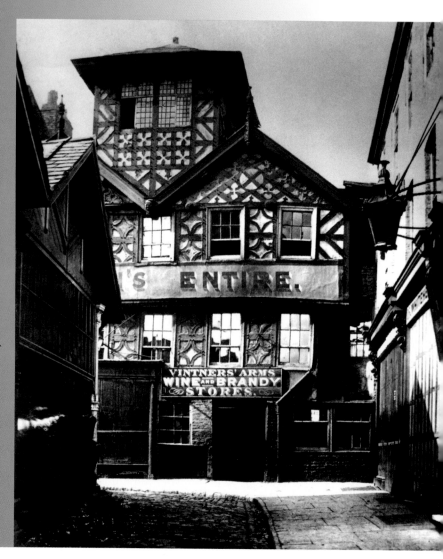

A Royal Occasion for Football

Looking down Mosley Street from Market Street, our image taken in 1866 shows the church of St. Peter's in the distance. St. Peter's was demolished in 1907 and the Cenotaph, created by Sir Edwin Lutyens, erected in its place in 1934.

On the corner of Mosley Street and Market Street was the Royal Hotel, the venue chosen by the Football Association to make the final decision concerning the first professional football league on 17 April 1888.

At this meeting it was decided that the division would include twelve clubs, except one of the clubs, Charterhouse, declined the invitation. Many of the founding clubs no longer exist or have moved into playing rugby union.

On the left of the picture is Hammond, Turners & Bates, a Manchester company renowned

or manufacturing buttons. In fact,
xamples of their buttons have
een found as far afield as on US
Confederate uniforms.

he Electric Telegraph Company
ounded in the UK in 1846 by John
ewis Ricardo and Sir William
othergill. Two years after our
hotograph in 1868 the Electric
elegraph Company became the
ritish General Post Office.

oday Mosley Street is still at the
eart of Manchester's thriving city life
nd even has its own tram station, on
he Altrincham–Eccles line.

Stretford's Pastoral Past

Stretford's origins as a village can be discovered in its name, comprising of the Anglo-Saxon 'straet' meaning street, and 'ford' denoting a crossing place, in this instance the River Mersey at Crossford Bridge.

During the early 1800s Stretford was one of the many towns surrounding Manchester instrumental in the early manufacture of cotton.

Many homes had handlooms where families had the opportunity to earn more money for the household rather than relying completely on farming as the principal trade.

However, by the end of the 1800s most of these cottage industries had disappeared due to rapid industrialisation of the cotton industry through the advancement in machinery in mills.

Our image dates from about 1870 showing the Cock Inn, a popular watering hole for carters and carriers on their way to and from Manchester. It was also the place for locals to meet, swap stories and gossip.

The country pub has been replaced, although the building is still being used to serve the local community as a newsagents shop. While the road seems to be just as wide as in our older picture, the mode of transport has altered dramatically from horse-drawn carts to cars.

The area in general has become far more industrialised with plenty of new businesses enjoying the easy links into the city. The pastoral days of Stretford's past appear to be long gone.

Manchester's First Free Library

Long Millgate, close to the entrance, to Chetham's Hospital, School and Library and Manchester Grammar School in 1875. These buildings have been an integral aspect of the city's architecture since the 1500s.

In 1518 Manchester's first Grammar School was constructed for the sum of £218 13s 5d at the request of Hugh Oldham. The school finally outgrew their original premises on Long Millgate and moved to Old Hall Lane.

Chetham's School and Library is comprised of buildings from several different periods, the earliest being from the 15th Century. Thomas de la Warre, Lord of Manchester, approached Henry V to gain permission to reform the church into a collegiate foundation in 1421.

Humphrey Chetham, a rich Manchester merchant, tried to purchase the site in order to establish a hospital and library. However, before Chetham could complete the purchase of the buildings he passed away, leaving instructions to his executors to complete the acquisition and establish a hospital and library on the premises. His will detailed that a hospital and school should be provided for forty poor boys giving them the opportunity for an education, and a healthier life.

Chetham's Library was the first free public library in England and has had many famous visitors over the years, including Karl Marx and Frederick Engels, who met at the library regularly prior to their publishing the 'Communist Manifesto' in 1848. Today Chetham's is known for its library and music school.

The buildings in the left foreground of our image formed part of the famous Poet's Corner, which included the Sun Inn where a group of Manchester poets including Charles Swain, William Rowlinson, John Critchley Prince, and Samuel Bamford used to meet.

After the devastation of the IRA bomb in 1996, the Long Millgate area has been altered and the space opened up to include the Cathedral Gardens.

Grand Garden Designs

Our image of the entrance to Alexandra Park dates from the early 20th Century.

Public parks were essentially a 19th-century invention, the idea being that they allowed workers the chance to escape the grudge, grime and grit of the workplace, as well as their even grimmer living conditions. Many parks were developed on land donated by wealthy landowners or industrialists, and the top landscape designers of the day were hired to create them.

Manchester opened its first public parks in 1846. Initially three parks were opened: Queen's Park, Philip's Park and Peel Park. Alexandra Park opened to the public in 1870 and the design of the park was left to Alexander Hennel. The original

arden design included a raised
rraced area lined with lime trees,
rnamental features and areas
esignated for sports. The park also
ecame a popular venue for people
o listen to music as brass bands
ecame a regular feature.

lexandra Park proved to be
xtremely popular with families and
as served by trams from across the
ty. Alexandra Road had tracks for
oth directions rather than a single
e with passing loops. However, the
se of carriages and motor vehicles
as prohibited within the park
rounds.

Today Alexandra Park is still used
by local residents who enjoy the
benefits of being able to walk through
the grounds or take part in a quick
football match. The park is also used
every year for the Caribbean Carnival
with brightly coloured processions,
food stalls, a fairground and craft
stalls.

Bustling Shops on Barlow Moor Road

It is hard to believe that over 100 years separates these images of Barlow Moor Road, Chorlton. The buildings have remained almost the same save for a few replacement windows and the change in the types of businesses now found on the high street.

Taken on 17 May 1900, our image shows shopkeepers and pedestrians lining up outside the shop fronts posing for the camera. The window signs clearly display the wares of each shop from a butchers to a fruitier; the shops appear to be thriving. Several of the young ladies appear to be in some sort of school uniform and preparing to continue riding their bicycles.

The young boy in the forefront of this photograph is holding a poster declaring the "Relief of Mafeking". At this time Britain and her empire were heavily engaged in a war in South Africa against the Dutch-speaking Boer republics. The Boers had proven

apable enemies inflicting a number of embarrassing defeats on Imperial orces. However, the news on the ay that this image was taken was of he relief of the British-held town of Mafeking which had been under siege or some time.

everal years later in the summer eason of 1908, Belle Vue Amusement Park made this battle he topic of one of their popular eenactments. They employed ormer soldiers and actors to reenact he main actions of the battle, filling he air with shouts and gunfire. The vening would usually finish with a uge firework display.

In our present day image there are no pedestrians or bicycles; instead they have been replaced by cars. Barlow Moor Road is still a busy road with plenty of shops, restaurants and direct links into the city.

Edwardian Monton Green

An Edwardian view of Monton Green Bridge, on the Bridgewater Canal, near Patricroft.

One of the narrow-beamed steam tugs can be seen chugging along and it appears that the photographer has attracted the attentions of the lady and the little girl.

The Bridgewater Canal was constructed by James Brindley at the instigation of the Duke of Bridgewater between 1759 and 1761. The canal made a significant difference to the industry of Manchester, ensuring that coal could be shipped to the mills and factories in the city in an efficient and economic manner.

By 1885, the canal that had been responsible for a revolution in transportation in Britain changed hands from the Bridgewater Navigation Company to the Manchester Ship Canal Company for the then staggering sum of £1,710,000.

A commercial barge can be seen in the background of our present day photograph, and despite competition from road and rail, commercial traffic continued to be carried on the system until 1974.

The Bridgewater Canal is still owned by the Manchester Ship Canal Company and the Bridgewater Canal Trust. The Trust was formed in 1971 in response to a breach of the canal at Dunham Massey in Altrincham. The Trust is made up of representatives from eight north-west county councils and the Manchester Ship Canal Company.

Today the canal is used for leisure purposes, whether you are on a narrow boat, walking or cycling alongside the canal towpath, or even fishing in the canal.

Magic at The Regent

This is the Cross Lane tramway junction in Salford near the intersection with Trafford Road, Regent Road, and Eccles New Road.

The photograph was taken in the early 1900s showing a bustling thoroughfare. A lone policeman watches the traffic and pedestrians pass by. By 1912 the large ornate pole dominating the centre of our image and supporting the overhead wires, was finally removed.

The large building on the left of our image is the Regent Theatre built by Frank Matcham and opened in 1895. The original name for the theatre was the Regent Theatre and Opera House, later known as the Regent Theatre of Varieties.

The theatre hosted a great many performers at this time including a visit from 'The Great Mysto'. He was an entertainer from Yorkshire who used a coffin as part of his act. 'Mysto' pushed his arms and legs through holes in the coffins sides, and his hands were manacled as the lid of the coffin was screwed into place.

'The Great Mysto' (otherwise known as Jim Pickles) was gaining popularity with his Edwardian audience until another competing escapologist, Harry Houdini, decided to publicly denounce his act by revealing to a shocked Regent Theatre audience exactly how the trick was performed.

The building that had witnessed so many performers underwent another alteration, became the Palace Theatre, and was eventually converted into a cinema though it retained the ability to stage live shows and theatre as required. The building was finally demolished in 1963 and the roadway was expanded to accommodate the increase in traffic through the area.

Monton Green's Railroad Past

The London & North Western route to Bolton and Wigan diverged from the Manchester – Liverpool main line at Patricroft, the first station on this line being Monton Green.

The line was used as one of the main links for the transportation of coal into Manchester.

Monton Green station was opened in 1887, providing a service for commuters enabling them to travel quickly into Manchester. The station finally closed on 5 May 1969 as part of the nationwide closures recommended by Dr Richard Beeching to reduce the costs of running the railway system in the country.

A colliery was sunk at Monton probably during the early-to-mid 1830s, and was located to the south

of what is now Monton Road. The pit was small, too small to make the construction of a tramway to the nearby Bridgewater Canal a viable option, coal mined from the site appeared to have been despatched by horse and cart.

This image taken in the early 1900s shows how traffic on the roads seems to be fairly quiet in Monton Green, as a horse appears to be enjoying the contents of its nose-bag in the middle of the street.

The church spire on the left of the picture is Monton Unitarian Church and was officially opened on 23 September 1875, although there have been other churches on the site since the 1600s. The first church built on this site was torn down by a Jacobite mob in 1715.

Today the railway line and the station have gone, and transportation from Monton Green into the city is primarily done by road.

Simon's Bridge

There are references to Northenden as far back as the Domesday Book. In 1086 the village was recognised as a small farming community with a manor house, woods and situated close to a ford on the River Mersey.

Anyone fording the river at Northenden had to walk diagonally across the river as the crossing points were not directly opposite each other. In 1901 an iron bridge known as Simon's Bridge was constructed across the river linking Northenden with Didsbury.

Our image taken in the early 1900s on Palatine Road shows a busy high street with one of the shops displaying its goods on the pavement. Although the shopping area is busy the roads are almost empty of traffic, as a lone horse and cart can be seen in the distance.

Palatine Road is so named because it provides one of the main road links between two county palatines, Cheshire and Lancashire. County palatines are areas that were once ruled by a court palatine, where an earl or duke was granted authority to rule that area independently of the king.

As Manchester continued to develop and expand, villages like Northenden also began to see shifts away from the rural life of the village towards more industrialised lifestyles. By 1909 a regular motorbus service was established between Church Road, Northenden and West Didsbury.

Today Northenden is a vibrant and busy shopping district filled with shops, restaurants, bars, take-away restaurants and travel agents. Quick transport links into Manchester along Palatine Road means that the street is constantly busy with cars, buses, bicycles and pedestrians. The rural village has truly disappeared and in its place a thriving business and residential area has emerged.

Brooks Bar Junction

Taken in the early 1900s on the corner of Withington Road and Upper Chorlton Road, and looking down Chorlton Road, our picture captures a street scene bereft of traffic.

People are enjoying a quiet walk down the street and perusing the contents of the shop windows.

As the picture shows, there used to be quite a complicated tramway layout at this junction, allowing tramcars to take any number of routes. The tramway system linking Oxford Road, Moss Lane East, Raby Street, Moss Lane West, Preston Street, Boston Street and Stretford Road was energised on 1 December 1902, the date when much of the city went over to electric trams. Chorlton Road and Upper Chorlton Road were energised on 13 April 1903.

Brooks Bar Junction, as this area has became known, is an unusual meeting point where five Manchester roads converge: Upper Chorlton Road, Shrewsbury Street Withington Road, Moss Lane West and Chorlton Road. The junction was named after local entrepreneur Samuel Brooks, a wealthy calico printer who was responsible for developing a lot of the land and housing for wealthy businessmen in the Whalley Range area at the end of the 19th Century. A toll-bar was built at Brook's Bar to guard the new exclusive estate of Victorian villas.

The former Brooks Bar Post and Telegraph Office building survives into our modern day image as a solicitor's office. The bank at the corner of Moss Lane West was replaced at some time with another building that occupies the same location.

Although the trams no longer run along these roads there is still a substantial amount of traffic as this junction carries nearly 9,000 passengers per day on the third busiest bus corridor in the Greater Manchester area.

Long Lost Station

Didsbury Station on Wilmslow Road as it looked in Midland Railway days. Situated 5.75 miles from Manchester Central, journey times to and from the city were between 12 and 17 minutes long.

The station was closed to goods traffic on 2 November 1964 and to passengers on 2 January 1967, the same day that passenger services ceased at Chorlton-cum-Hardy station.

A Hansom cab, as seen on the far left, is one of the various horse-drawn vehicles pictured here outside the station. Cab fares were regulated and could be booked by the mile or by the hour. In 1910 it cost 9d per mile for 1-2 people sharing and a shilling per mile if 3-4 shared. For each additional third of a mile there was a charge of 3-4d. If booked by the hour the cab price was 2/6d; you would

be charged more for each additional quarter of an hour. For each article of luggage carried outside there was a charge of 2d, and fares doubled from midnight to 6.00am. Electric trams were much cheaper with fares ranging from 1d to 3d per journey.

Didsbury Station was eventually demolished and the site redeveloped to make way for lively restaurants and bars. The combination of speciality shops and vibrant nightlife make Didsbury one of the most sought after places to live in the Greater Manchester area.

A Lost Late-Georgian Gem

One of Manchester's lost late-Georgian architectural gems St. Matthew's Church was once found on Liverpool Road, off Deansgate.

The church was designed in 1825 by arguably the most famous architect of his time, Sir Charles Barry, renowned for designing the Houses of Parliament. The church was constructed between Higher and Lower Campfield Markets.

The 165ft-high slender tower and spire dominated the skyline of Liverpool Road for many years before the church was finally demolished in 1951. The bell from the tower was removed in 1947 and given to St. Anne's Church in Belfield.
Two other notable buildings designed by Sir Charles Barry are the Manchester City Art Gallery and the Athenaeum.

Today the only part of the church that still exists is the grade II listed former Sunday School, which has since been converted into offices. In the background of our modern image looms the impressive 48-storey Beetham Tower, also known as the Hilton Tower.

The 554ft tower designed by Ian Simpson Architects accommodates the four-star Hilton hotel on the first 23 storeys and the remaining storeys are comprised of residential apartments, including a penthouse apartment owned by the architect Ian Simpson.

Shopping Delights in Moss Side

Moss Side at the turn of the 19th Century was a small rural village, where the main source of employment was found in farming and agriculture.

The Industrial Revolution changed the village beyond all recognition as more and more people came to Manchester seeking work in the mills and factories. Moss Side developed rapidly to meet the housing needs of commuters and factory workers. New grid pattern streets were designed to allow the maximum amount of back-to-back terraces to be fit into some areas, while other streets had a more open feel to them

Our image on Alexandra Road, Moss Side, was taken in the early 1900s. The street is quite wide, allowing for tramlines to be accommodated, and still leaving enough room for cars and

icycles to navigate the street.

Vhile one side of the street appears
o be residential the other side seems
o be one long line of shops. Notably
n the left of the picture is an agent
or various railway companies,
ncluding Cheshire Lines Committee
nd the Lancashire and Yorkshire
nes.

On the right of the picture, Noddings
Chemist shop on the corner has a
uge advertisement for Hyde's Ales
 Stouts, the Manchester brewery,
n the front of the building. Most of
he shops have awnings extending
ver the pavement, offering their

customers either shade or shelter
depending on the weather.

Moss Side has undergone extensive
redevelopment over the years
with many of the old Victorian and
Edwardian houses demolished and
replaced by modern housing.

Billiards on Washway Road

In the early 1900s the village of Sale was prospering; the industrialisation of Manchester had meant that the area had witnessed a substantial increase in housing and employment.

Excellent transportation links by rail and road meant that Sale was an ideal location for wealthy merchants and businessmen who needed to be within commuting distance of the city

Our image of Washway Road, Sale, taken in the early 1900s, shows two policemen in the centre of the street standing on the tram tracks with only a horse-drawn cart as traffic on the road. There are several shops with pedestrians lingering by the window displays.

The advertisement on the side of a building for the Palace of Varieties and Worsley Historical Pageant are

an indication of the amusements available to locals. The Billiard Hall pictured on the right of the image is another example of how society was moving towards a balance between work and leisure activities, as workers had more free time and disposable income.

Billiards had become a popular sport for men and women of all classes. However, billiard halls were usually the exclusive domain of men.

Historically there are references to the game being played in the 15th Century by kings, queens and courtiers alike, and there are also references to the game in Shakespeare's *Antony and Cleopatra*.

By the 1900s the game had progressed significantly with a standardisation of the form and rules of the game. Billiards proved to be a popular game and equally many people also enjoyed making wagers on the outcome of the play whether they were the players or spectators.

Leisure activities have continued to develop, and billiard halls are no longer as popular as they used to be. Many of the halls that were built throughout Manchester have either been demolished or converted into different uses.

Today the former billiard hall on Washway Road remains, but the usage of the building has changed to a store. The road no longer has tramlines but there are plenty of cars and buses that continue to use the route.

The Changing Face of Longsight Market

This busy Edwardian street scene was taken in the early 1900s on Stockport Road, Longsight, with Dickenson Road joining Stockport Road at the crossroad.

Shoppers throng both sides of the street, and passengers laden with parcels can be seen waiting to step onto the tram heading to Manchester The horse-drawn vehicle on the left of the image outside Boots the Chemist appears to be a dairy float, the milk being dispensed from a large churn by a measuring can.

The bank building on the left of our image on the corner of Stockport Road and Dickenson Road is one of the only remaining buildings linking the two photographs together, although nearly 100 years have passed. Left of the bank building down Dickenson Road is the vibrant

nd busy Longsight Market. The
market place continues to thrive
with a wide variety of stalls providing
plenty of fresh produce.

Longsight Market is also used as
the venue for Chand Raat, where
the local community have the
opportunity to celebrate the night
before Eid with bhangra dancing,
music, food and craft stalls.

Stockport Road continues to be one
of the busiest roads into Manchester
from Stockport. The mix of shops
and eating establishments along
Stockport Road illustrate Longsight's
increasingly multicultural community

with a selection of restaurants and
cafés ranging from Indian cuisine
through to Caribbean.

Manchester's Medical Past

Manchester Royal Infirmary's humble beginnings in a small 12-bed house in Withy Grove in 1752 bears little resemblance to the 800-bed hospital it has become today.

A purpose-built infirmary, designed to provide treatment for those unable to pay, opened on Lever's Row, Piccadilly, in 1755.

In 1765 the Lunatic Hospital opened on an adjacent site, and remained there for eighty years until it moved to a new location in Cheadle. The vacated property was immediately acquired and absorbed into the infirmary. Over the years the infirmary was remodelled and expanded one wing is said to have been paid for out of the proceeds of a concert given by the great Jenny Lind, a Swedish born opera singer of the 1800s.

Though many Manchester patients were too poor to pay for their treatments, they were seen by some of the most outstanding medical practitioners of the age.

One such talented late-Victorian surgeon was Oldham-born Walter Whitehead. He can best be described as having an unusual approach to some of his surgical procedures, and is famous for removing a cancerous tongue with a pair of scissors.

The Royal Infirmary at Piccadilly Gardens closed in 1908 and moved to new premises on Oxford Road, close to the Royal Manchester Eye Hospital. The new building was officially opened by King Edward VII and Queen Alexandra in 1909.

Medical Science has undergone significant changes since the first hospital in Manchester was opened, throughout the decades Manchester had continued to remain at the forefront of medical research and development.

Victoria's Changing Fortunes

Victoria Station was originally built in 1844, offering a small single platform for the Manchester-Leeds trans-Pennine railway.

By the 1880s the station underwent significant redevelopment by George Stephenson, who designed a 700ft iron and glass train shed.

Our image, taken in the early 1920s, features a Lancashire & Yorkshire steam locomotive standing at the station with a platform full of passengers waiting to embark.

Victoria was one of Manchester's main line stations and from here it was possible to reach the likes of York; Scarborough via Normanton or Leeds; Windermere via Preston; Fleetwood, as well as local services to Accrington, Bolton, Bury, Middleton,

ochdale, and Burnley.

ctoria survived the railway
tionalisation of the 1960s and 70s
ough both Manchester Central
nd Manchester Exchange did close.
he closure of Exchange Station also
onsigned to history the UK's longest
assenger platform, shared with
ctoria, that was 2,194ft long.

1996 sections of Victoria Station
ere badly damaged by the IRA
omb blast in Manchester city centre.
luch of the glasswork and the
dwardian façade to the station have
een repaired and replaced due to
e extent of the damage.

The Metrolink system in Manchester
took over former British Rail tracks,
a consequence of which was the
remodelling of part of Victoria to
allow metro-trams from Bury to gain
access to the city centre and the
route to Altrincham.

Portland Street and its Cotton Past

Looking down Portland Street from Oxford Street there is plenty of activity apparent in this 1920s image of Manchester.

The pavements are bustling with pedestrians and the road is crammed with lorries, trams and horse-drawn vehicles. On the left of the picture is Manchester's Berlitz School of Languages, established in the early 1900s.

In the distance stands J & S Watts' warehouse, better known today as the Britannia Hotel, where over one thousand people were employed. The building, designed by architects Travis and Mangnall's in 1851-6, was originally used as a home trade warehouse.

hese warehouses were used to
market products in a luxurious
setting to retailers and wealthy
homeowners alike. Watt's warehouse
was designed to include 23 bays
(approximately 300ft long) and six
storeys (nearly 100ft high) each floor
was designed individually in order to
display the goods in the best setting.

Designs were opulent and colourful,
highlighting each piece to entice the
buyers. The warehouse displayed
styles ranging from Italian chic to
the sultry indulgence of an Egyptian
palace.

Portland Street remains one of
Manchester's busiest thoroughfares
with a constant stream of traffic at
all hours of the day and night. The
impressive warehouses that once
showcased fine cloths produced in
Manchester's mills in the 1800s have
since been converted into hotels and
modern office complexes.

Chorlton's Tram Terminus

Chorlton-cum-Hardy became a suburb of the city of Manchester in 1904. The continuing improvements in transportation links between the village and the city were ideal for commuters.

This photograph, taken in the 1920s on the corner of Barlow Moor Road and Malton Avenue, shows a fair amount of activity at Chorlton tram terminus. Car 775 is on the number 13 route; Hightown and Chorlton-cum-Hardy via Albert Square, All Saints, Chorlton Road, and Banks's Bar. Car 391 is on the number 54 route; Chorlton and Hightown via Seymour Grove, Chester Road and Great Ducie Street.

The number 13 route was converted to buses in June 1939 but reverted to trams in November 1942 following a request from the Regional Transport Commissioner for Manchester

Corporation to reduce bus mileage and petrol consumption. From 11 February 1945 tram services to Chorlton were reduced to peak hours as petrol buses took over once more.

Today the old terminus is still recognisable and is now being used by the Manchester Diving Group. The junction of Barlow Moor Road and Malton Avenue is still a busy intersection for traffic. Chorlton remains one of Manchester's more popular commuter suburbs with its mixture of shops, restaurants and sports facilities.

King Street's Banking Heritage

King Street was once home to a number of banks and insurance companies which formed the heart of Manchester's financial district. Our picture from the 1920s is dominated by Lloyds Bank on the corner of Cross Street.

The bank was designed in an Edwardian Baroque style by architects Charles Heathcote & Sons and completed in 1915. Heathcote was responsible for designing several buildings in Manchester including the Manchester University Dental Hospital on Bridgeford Street.

Next along is the District Bank (a forerunner of Natwest) built on the site of the York Hotel and then Royal London Insurance building which dates from the early 1860s. Lloyds was built on the site formerly occupied by Manchester's first Town Hall, designed by Francis Goodwin who is said to have derived the Grecian-Ionic style from the Erechtheum in Athens. The whole ensemble cost £41,971 and remained the seat of local government until replaced by Alfred Waterhouse's Gothic masterpiece in Albert Square.

The old Town Hall was then used to house Manchester's Free Library's reference department, a role it filled until 1912 when structural surveys revealed that the place was deteriorating rapidly and was subsequently demolished. The library meanwhile was removed and given 'temporary accommodation', a group of huts on one corner of Piccadilly, where it remained until 1934.

Today King Street is one of Manchester's principal streets for designer stores including Vivienne Westwood, Emporio Armani, Karen Millen, Ralph Lauren and Whistles.

Trams on Princess Parkway

February 1947, though certain trams continued to trundle over the route at peak hours only for a little longer.

The trams and buses allowed local residents access to Alexandra Park where they had the opportunity to spend their leisure time.

Princess Parkway remains one of the busiest roadways into Manchester city centre. The dual carriageway carries thousands of commuters into the city on a daily basis.

The planning and development of Princess Road, or Princess Parkway as it is more commonly known, occurred in the 1920s opening the southern part of Manchester and its suburbs to commuters.

If you have ever wondered why sections of Princess Parkway are blessed with grassed or tree-covered central reservations the answer is: it's where the tram tracks used to be.

Pictured here on the number 40 route, 18 October 1937, is car 226, one of four cars from batch 187-237 built in 1901 that were still being used in the Manchester fleet at the end of the Second World War. The number 40, East Didsbury via Kingsway, Birchfield Road, Albert Square and Princess Parkway to Barlow Moor Road converted to buses on 2

The Gateway

The development of Kingsway began in the 1920s as urban and road planning in Manchester underwent significant developments.

In this section of Kingsway at Parrs Wood the original area underwent extensive housing developments of semi-detached homes that can be seen along the road.

By the time our picture, dating from 30 July 1936, was taken the Gateway Hotel was under construction at the corner of Kingsway and Wilmslow Road, East Didsbury. Traffic amounts to just eight cars and vans, a handful of bicycles, a couple of handcarts, steam road-roller and a motorcyclist stopped in the middle of the road for a chat.

Traffic has continued to build over the decades and a footbridge was built across the main road to allow pedestrians to safely cross the road. Today the area has been redeveloped into a huge cinema complex, restaurant area, bowling alley and fitness centre.

There is also a fine example of an Art Deco apartment complex that dominates the opposite side of the road to the cinema. This junction is one of the busiest in South Manchester, with roads leading to Cheadle, Burnage, Heaton Mersey, Handforth, Didsbury and access to the M56 motorway.

Long Lost Victoria Buildings

The triangular-shaped Victoria Buildings were an integral part of a major city centre redevelopment in the 1860s and 70s.

This included the widening of the roads between St. Mary's Gate and Peter Street, Victoria Street to St. Mary's Gate, and the demolition of the last remnants of Smithy Door.

The building itself cost £140,000 to construct and comprised ground floor shops, office accommodations and the Victoria Hotel. There was also the Victoria Arcade that ran through the centre of the complex, while the middle of the building, officially described as a 'bazaar', had balconies running round it.

The number of shops and offices seems to have varied over the years

as has the number of rooms in the hotel. Some sources state that the hotel had 231 rooms yet in 1920, when it was one of only two RAC appointed hotels in the whole of Manchester, it is listed as having only 130 beds. The hotel's billiard room is reported to have had fifteen tables.

Our image, taken in the 1930s, shows the huge display windows for the store, showcasing a rich variety of goods for Mancunians to purchase. During the Second World War the building was so badly damaged during the Christmas Blitz of 1940 that it had to be demolished.

Today, high-rise tower blocks and the famous No.1 Deansgate apartment are on the site of the old Victoria Buildings. Designed by Ian Simpson Architects, this building cost £20 million to build and is seen as an icon of the regeneration Manchester City centre has undergone since the IRA bombing in 1996.

Trafford Park's Stately Past

Trafford Hall is one of the lost manorial houses of Manchester, having been demolished during the Second World War.

The older parts of the hall dated from the 16th Century, and when the house was extended in the 1760s the older part housed the servants' quarters, kitchen, bakery, brewery and dairy. The extension followed the fashion of the day and was completed in the Classical style, including a pediment supported on four Corinthian columns. It featured eight main reception rooms and a private Catholic chapel complete with five stained glass windows.

The beginning of the end for Trafford Hall and its estate, covering nearly 1,200 acres, came with the announcement that Manchester was

to be linked to the sea by a ship canal. Sir Humphrey de Trafford decided to place the estate up for sale and though Sir Humphrey died before the canal was finished, his son, another Sir Humphrey, continued to dispose of estate assets and sold more land.

In May 1896 the hall and over 1,100 acres were auctioned off at the Grand Hotel, Manchester. The buyer was Derbyshire-based financier and speculator Ernest Hooley who paid £36,000 for the lot and then proceeded to sell on most of the land to Trafford Park Estates for a massive £900,000.

At one point 80 acres of land nearest the hall were let to the Manchester Golf Club, which was also given access to part of the hall for use as a club-house. It was a popular move for the club as membership soared by nearly 400 per cent.

The sale of the land to Trafford Park Estates would forever change the landscape of the area. If the land had not been sold it would almost certainly have meant no Trafford Park Industrial Estate, and those early companies, such as the Ford Motor Company, may have decided to set up warehouses in another part of the country. Today the green fields and

impressive estate house have gone and in its place are industrial units and roadways.

Paulden's Department Store

In 1865 William Paulden, the son of a Knutsford farmer, decided to embark upon a life in retail rather than farming and set about opening a shop opposite St Mary's, Hulme.

William's first shop was a small affair, but business was good and by the end of 1868 he had acquired the three adjoining premises. The business continued to grow and eventually the firm moved into a large store on Stretford Road.

Our image, taken in 1933, shows the windows as they looked after Paulden's window dressers had done away with 'top-dressing' for the very first time. Apparently 'top-dressing' was the practice of sticking merchandise to the window itself by means of gummed stickers.

On 8 September 1957 crowds flocked to Paulden's Department Store to witness the devastating fire that claimed several lives. The fire began on the first floor, and despite valiant efforts by the Manchester Fire Brigade, who deployed firemen and all available machinery to the scene, it spread quickly engulfing the premises and leaving it gutted in less than three hours.

Needing a new home, Paulden's was lucky enough to take over the Rylands Building, a massive six-storey wholesale and retail warehouse occupying the prime site of 109-127 Market Street.

Today, Debenhams department store is on the site of the demolished Paulden's in the heart of Manchester's busy shopping district.

Piccadilly Gardens

Piccadilly was acquired by the Council, along with the old Manchester Royal Infirmary (MRI) building, for £400,000 following the MRI's move to its new site on Oxford Road in 1908.

Prior to the demolition of the hospital in 1910 the Council decided that any future building on the site would be limited to the area about to be cleared.

Our image taken on 14 July 1934 is of Manchester Reference Library's 'temporary' accommodation in Piccadilly. This was also the year the city's purpose-built Central Library in St. Peter's Square opened. In the background is the famous Lewis's sign advertising one of Manchester's premier department stores.

During the Second World War much of Piccadilly Gardens was converted into air-raid shelters and allotments. During the blitz on Manchester in December 1940 Piccadilly Gardens suffered a lot of damage as buildings around the square were severely bombed.

Today Piccadilly Gardens is an oasis of green in the heart of the city centre. The grounds have been part of a huge urban redevelopment programme, with the area being redesigned by renowned landscape architect Tadao Ando, featuring fountains and gardens. The original statues are still placed around the Gardens, and during the Christmas celebrations an ice-rink is set up for all to enjoy.

Blitz Damage Closes Courts

Built at a cost in excess of £100,000, the Assize Courts must have been an imposing sight when first completed. The main entrance was on the west side and was adorned with statues of eminent law-givers sculpted by Thomas Woolner; these statues included Moses, who was placed on the apex of the gable. At the building's centre stood a 210ft-high slender tower. Perhaps its most famous feature was its central hall, 100ft long, 48ft wide and 75ft high. At the north end of the hall was a stained glass window depicting the signing of the Magna Carta.

Our image, taken on the morning of 2 June 1941, shows the Assize Courts as a charred, smouldering ruin beyond salvation. The building was subsequently demolished, though many of the fine statues that had once adorned it were salvaged and can be seen to this day exhibited in the Crown Court building in Crown Square.

Today the area once occupied by Manchester's Assize Court is now Strangeway's Prison Visitor Centre.

On the night of 1 June 1941, the Luftwaffe attacked Manchester, delivering what would be the city's third heaviest raid of the war.

Locally, the raid is also remembered for the destruction it caused in Salford where fourteen nurses were killed when their home at the Salford Royal Infirmary was hit. The Reverend James Hussey of St. Phillip's Church was also killed by a bomb as he made his way to the nurses' home to comfort the wounded.

As daylight broke over Manchester firefighters were still hard at work. One of the battles they lost was the one to save the Assize Courts, architect Alfred Waterhouse's great Gothic Revival masterpiece of the 1860s. The building had influenced other architects including Edward Solomon's design for the Reform Club in King Street, and Thomas Worthington's designs for Minshull Street Courts, the Ellen Wilkinson High School, Hyde Road and the Memorial Hall in Albert Square.

The 'Last' Tram

By New Year 1949 Manchester Corporation Tramways' once extensive system had been reduced to just one route, the No.35 Exchange-Hazel Grove, which was jointly operated with Stockport.

The tram fleet that had once numbered close to 1,000 cars had been reduced to just 35.

On 9 January this route was converted to motorbus operation ar the following morning just five trams were employed during the morning rush hour. Afterwards four of the car took part in a closing procession with No.1007 bringing up the rear as the official last tram.

In our picture, people look on and a policeman gives a salute as No.1007 negotiates the junction at Slade Lane As the official last tram No.1007 carried the Lord Mayor, Alderman

Mary Kingsmill Jones, and other civic dignitaries.

All 35 trams met an ignominious end as not one was saved for preservation. They were taken to Hyde Road depot and destroyed in a controlled fire by the Manchester Fire Brigade on 16 March 1949.

The buildings on the left have survived to today, though during the intervening years businesses have come and gone and the roadway has undergone a slight realignment.

London Road Fire Station

During the first decade of the 20th Century, the Baroque style was all the rage among architects commissioned to design Manchester's public buildings, including the Royal Infirmary at Chorlton-on-Medlock, Parr's Bank in Spring Gardens, the Lancashire and Yorkshire Railway's Victoria Station, and London Road Fire Station.

A competition was held for the design of the fire station and judged by the renowned architect Alfred Waterhouse. The winners were Woodhouse, Willoughby & Langham who proposed a stunning triangular-shaped building in red Accrington brick and terracotta. It was opened by the Lord Mayor on 27 September 1906 and the fire station was without doubt one of the finest municipal

buildings in the UK.

In 1906 the Manchester Fire Brigade was an integrated part of the city police force, a common practice in this period, the firemen also being warranted police officers with powers of arrest. It was therefore not surprising that this magnificent building also housed a police station as well as a coroner's court, an ambulance station, and the Weights & Measures Department. Along one side of a large open area was the accommodation block for 32 men, their wives and children, and additional room was available for six unmarried men.

When the station first opened, the Manchester Fire Brigade was still using horse-drawn appliances, though these were in the process of being replaced with motorised equipment. In fact, the first motorised fire appliance had been constructed by the Protector Lamp & Lighting Company in 1901 at their workshops in Monton, near Eccles.

In recent years there have been plans for turning the building into a hotel and office complex but so far the premises have largely remained unused and empty. Since the 1980s parts of the building have been used for storage.

Transport in Piccadilly Gardens

Half a century separates these images of Piccadilly Gardens but each shows how the area has remained a hub for transportation links in the city centre.

Our image from 1957 shows covered bus stands and passengers patiently waiting for a ride home.

By the 1950s, the tramway system in Manchester had finally been phased out, and buses and trains remained the main public transportation services for people travelling around the area.

Lewis's Department Store can be seen in the background of the image and was one of Manchester's premier stores and landmarks through the decades. The sign was eventually replaced by the Primark department store sign when the company took

over ownership of the building.

Piccadilly Gardens is Manchester's main open inner-city garden area, surrounded by buildings that reflect the changing architectural history of the city, from Victorian brick buildings to more modern glass and steel constructions.

The Gardens have been completely remodelled and are still one of Manchester's central gathering points. In summer, workers are able to enjoy sitting in the sun, and during the winter the gardens are transformed to include an outdoor ice-skating rink.

Today Piccadilly is the hub of Manchester's reinstated tram system - the Metrolink - where routes from Altrincham, Eccles and Bury converge. The bus shelter is no longer there although there are still bus stops where passengers can catch buses.

Buile Hill Park

Buile Hill Park in Pendleton, Salford, became a grade II listed park of national historic importance in 2001. Our image, taken in the 1950s, shows a local man enjoying a walk in the peaceful tree-lined park.

Originally the Buile Hill Mansion and Estate was built in 1825 for Manchester's Lord Mayor, Sir Thomas Potter. The house, designed by the famous architect Sir Charles Barry, who was also responsible for designing the Houses of Parliament, the Athenaeum in Manchester and Manchester City Art Gallery.

Salford and Manchester Councils' were instrumental in developing urban planning to include city parks. Salford Council opened Peel Park in 1846, Albert Park in 1877, Ordsall Park in 1879, and in 1902 purchased Buile Hall and its adjoining land. It opened as a public park the following year, and the hall itself was converted to house Salford's Museum of Natural History by 1906.

Buile Hill Park continued to develop over the decades and even played its part in the war effort during the Second World War. In 1939 the parks office was requisitioned and used as the headquarters for the C Flight of the RAF Balloon Barrage. During the blitz of the Salford area in 1940 a bomb was dropped on the hall but thankfully did not cause any significant damage. During the war years even the park's fencing was taken for melting down into bullets. By the end of the war in 1945, Buile Hill Park seemed to be the perfect place to hold VE Day celebrations.

By the 1950s normalcy was returning to the park, and the post war years saw many new developments in the amenities available to locals in the park, including the redevelopment of the Conservatory and a petting zoon for children.

In 1975 the Museum of Natural History closed and was replaced by the Salford Museum of Mining. The museum finally closed in 2000 and plans for re-developing the park are firmly underway as new play areas for children, bowling greens, tennis courts and spaces allowing for funfairs have been constructed for the enjoyment of local residents.

Deansgate

Deansgate is one of Manchester's primary roads, running north-south along the western part of the city.

The northern end of Deansgate runs parallel with the River Irwell and has undergone significant redevelopments due to the IRA bombing in 1996, including the construction of the award winning building containing Manchester's most exclusive penthouse - No.1 Deansgate.

Our view of Deansgate taken in the late 1950s shows a familiar view of the Art Deco frontage of Kendals (House of Fraser) Department Store on the right of the image. As always the traffic flow on Deansgate is busy even on this wet and stormy day, with a combination of cars, lorries and double-decker buses on the road.

The rain still doesn't stop people from shopping, armed with their umbrellas pedestrians move from shop to shop along the street.

Off in the distance on the right is one of Deansgate's more famous buildings, the grade I listed John Rylands Library. Architect Sir Basil Champneys was commissioned by Mrs Enriqueta Rylands, a native of Cuba, in memory of her late husband, north-west entrepreneur John Ryland. The red-brick Victorian Neo-Gothic library is home to a collection of rare manuscripts and books, including most notably, exquisite illuminated medieval manuscripts and personal papers of literary greats such as Elisabeth Gaskell and John Wesley.

Deansgate is also known for its eclectic range of restaurants, cafés and bars offering a selection to suit anyone's mood and appetite. Barton's Arcade is a grade II listed Victorian cast iron and glass construction which links Deansgate with St. Ann's Square. The arcade offers a combination of boutiques, coffee shops and office suites to tempt customers and workers alike.

A Theatre's Industrial Past

When our picture was taken in the early 1960s the trading floor of the Royal Exchange was still in business, although the cotton trade was in decline.

When King George V officially opened the building's new extension on 8 October 1921 the extension included a post office, cable office and commercial library. In the early 1920s more than 2,000 firms were represented here and there were well over 11,000 individual members. By the early 1930s the cotton industry was suffering from the combined effects of the US recession, foreign competition and the boycott of British cotton by the Indian Congress Party as part of their campaign for Indian independence. This was a significant blow to the industry as India was one of our biggest customers.

By 1968 there were so few members left that continued operation of the exchange was no longer viable. Some, though by no means all, had gone

bust and many had amalgamated into larger organisations.

The Exchange then stood empty for five years until the Sixty-Nine Theatre Company leased it as a temporary venue. It wasn't long before someone came up with the idea that perhaps the building could be modified and a permanent theatre established.

In 1976 a group of artistic directors - including Casper Wrede, Richard Negri, Michael Elliott, Braham Murray and James Maxwell – founded the Royal Exchange Theatre. During the IRA bombing of Manchester in 1996 the theatre was badly damaged and was forced to close for two years as the building underwent extensive re-development costing £32 million.

The Royal Exchange Theatre, reopened by Prince Edward on 30 November 1998, has proven to be incredibly successful, attracting a high calibre of actors to appear on its stage, including Helen Mirren, Albert Finney, Kate Winslett, Vanessa Redgrave and Tom Courtenay.

Cheadle's Turnpike Past

One of the first records of Cheadle Village is in the Domesday Book of 1086 when the village was said to be worth 10 shillings.

The manor continued to grow in influence and wealth, and by the 14th Century the village had two corn mills, Higher Mill and Lower Mill.

By the 18th Century the newly formed Turnpike Trust undertook the maintenance of the road from Didsbury to Wilmslow via Cheadle.

New stone bridges were constructed over the River Mersey and Micker Brook, and in anticipation of the increased traffic along this highway, two new coaching inns were also established: The George & Dragon and The White Hart both of which are still in use today.

During the 1960s Cheadle Village underwent significant redevelopment as many of the residential properties around Andrew Street, Church Street, Massie Street, Charles Street and the Chapel Street area were demolished to make way for car parking areas. The new car parks were seen as a mark of how the village was continuing to prosper.

Our image taken in the 1960s shows a busy Cheadle High Street with the grade II listed George & Dragon coaching inn on the left of the picture. In the distance can be seen the grade I listed, 16th-century St. Mary's Church, a local landmark.

Today Cheadle Village High Street is bustling with cars, buses and shoppers. There has been little change in the shop fronts, although notably the Ockleston Memorial Fountain on the right of the 1960s picture has been moved to Queens Gardens, and the road widened slightly to allow for traffic.

Long Gone Flower Street

Chimney pots, gas lamps, cobbles and rubble, yet no gardens or flowers can be seen on Flower Street, Ancoats, on this dismal day in January 1962. The factory lights of the mill in the background beckon workers to their jobs.

Ancoats was at the heart of Manchester's Industrial Revolution, with huge cotton mills being erected in the area. The mills were at the centre of the city's industrial life and plenty of houses were soon constructed for workers near to the sites. These houses were basic two-up-two-down constructions, with the front door opening directly onto the street, and in many cases the backyards were shared areas where families had to share outside toilet facilities.

In 1954 new legislation enabled the Council to take a fresh look at its housing needs. The result was a five-

year plan to demolish and replace 7,500 slums, some of them among the worst in the entire UK. Flower Street has been one of the streets consigned to history as the old houses were demolished to make room for new builds.

Many of the old mills went into disrepair once cotton ceased to be the main source of income in the area. Since then, the buildings have had changing fortunes, some being used for other industrial purposes, others for simple storage facilities. However, in recent years many of these brick-built remnants of Manchester's industrial past have been granted grade II listing.

These red-brick Ancoats giants witnessed the daily grind of Manchester's commerce from fruit, vegetable, fish and ice products to the manufacture of cotton. Today developers are keen to invest in these buildings, modernising the interiors into new offices and apartment complexes.

Changing Fortunes of Urmston

There has been a town at Urmston, or as it was originally known Orme's Tun (dwelling), since medieval times.

The land comprising Orme's Tun was originally gifted to Orme, the son of Edward Aylward, under the reign of King John, who ruled between 1199 and 1216.

The family of de Ormeston built Urmston Old Hall c1350 in the area that is known today as Manor Avenue. Although the original hall was demolished, a new brick and timber construction was built in the 16th Century. The hall later became a farm and was finally demolished in 1937.

The small farming community changed beyond all recognition during the Industrial Revolution when the railway lines were extended, and a station was built in Urmston providing commuters with the means of transport to travel into the city.

Just over forty years separates our two pictures of Station Road, Urmston, the older image being taken in February 1966. The street seems quite quiet although there are plenty of shops on either side of the road.

In recent years Urmston's shopping area has undergone some hardship due to the opening of the famous Trafford Centre, a large shopping and leisure complex north of the town. However there are plans to re-develop Urmston's shopping centre and Trafford Borough Council has identified it as a priority regeneration area.

Cross Street News

The van outside the building would have been one of a fleet used to transport the latest edition of the newspaper to local newsagents. There is also a newsstand outside the building designed to catch the eye of pedestrians as they walk down the street. The *Manchester Evening News* finally moved to new premises on Deansgate, and this grand building was eventually demolished to make way for more modern buildings.

Today Cross Street is still home to several financial companies, as can be seen in our image, although unusually the street appears to be deserted of traffic. Across the road from where the *Manchester Evening News* offices used to be is the Royal Exchange Theatre.

Cross Street is well known for its architecture, including two notable financial buildings designed in the Edwardian Baroque style by architect Charles Heathcote: the Eagle Star House constructed in 1911, and Lloyds Bank in 1915.

Our image of the red-brick Victorian *Manchester Evening News* building at No.3 Cross Street was taken on 18 April 1966 and shared the building with the *Manchester Guardian* prior to the paper's move to London. To the left of the picture is No.1 Cross Street, home of the *Manchester Courier* newspaper, which operated there between 1825 and 1915.

Ragged School Past

The area known locally as St. Michael's Flags was the site formerly occupied by the church of St. Michael and All Angels, and the 'New Burying Ground'.

The church's own burial ground had closed in 1854, and in 1890 had been handed over to the city for use as a playground. The 'New Burying Ground' was consecrated in 1787 and was described as "the largest cemetery in the town appropriated to the internment of poor persons who have no family place of burial." There were so many dead that the coffins were stacked in rows and on top of each other in large pits and by 1816 the grounds were full.

St. Michael's Church had been built by Humphrey Owen in 1788 and at one time stood in a delightful neighbourhood. The nearby Ashley

Lane ran through fields to Ashley Woods and Collyhurst Woods, and the stream still ran with clear water. But times change and Angel Meadow, the parish served by the church, became the most notorious in Manchester, a place of foul slums, crime, and prostitution.

Our image of St. Michael's Flags, taken in October 1967, shows the Charter Street Ragged School and Working Girls' Home' and a railway bridge in the background. This school was opened in 1892, although there had been other industrial schools on the site since 1847. The school provided clothes, food, clogs, medical services and the chance for the children to learn basic literacy and practical skills such as carpentry.

Today the area that was once covered in burial flags is now a local park with open spaces and meandering footpaths. The Ragged School is still being used as a teaching facility for a mixed boys and girls independent school.

Picture House Consigned to Past

This image of the Oxford Street Cinema, once known as the Oxford Street Picture House, dates from August 1968.

This red-brick and terracotta building is one of the old cinema buildings that once thronged Oxford Street and has since been converted into other uses.

The advertising on the outside of the cinema is for two movies: The Fabulous Adventures of Marco Polo, and Apaches Last Battle. The Marco Polo movie started in 1962 but wasn't finished until 1963 due to lack of funding. It featured an all-star cast with Horst Buchholz as Marco Polo and Anthony Quinn as Kublai Khan.

oaches Last Battle otherwise
own in the USA as Old
atterhand, featured Lex Barker as
d Shatterhand.

uring the 1960s and 1970s many
Manchester's old cinemas were
rced to close. Some of them had
len into severe states of disrepair
hilst others could not compete with
e new multi-screen cinemas that
ere being built.

day the building still retains
mnants of its 'Picture House' past,
th the old cinema signs clearly
ible above the modern signage
the building's current fast-food

occupant, McDonald's. The front of
the building has been cleaned and
renovated to reveal the beautiful lines
of the original design.

St. Mary's Gate Woolworth's

Woolworth's might never have become a household name in America and the UK if Franklin Winfield Woolworth had given up after his first store in Utica, New York, failed.

However, in 1879 he opened up a new store, this time in Lancaster, Pennsylvania.

Woolworth's philosophy was simple: buy in cheap and sell it on cheap. All items were priced at either five or ten cents each. It was a success and soon Franklin's brother Charles had joined him in the business, and over the coming decades branches were opened across the USA and in Canada, many in collaboration with other partners.

Woolworth's first UK outlet was opened in Liverpool in 1909 and the Manchester store was opened the

llowing year. Our image, taken on
9 March 1971, shows Manchester's
. Mary's Gate store that had
een scheduled for closure due to
development. Woolworth's other
ain store in Manchester at the time
as on the corner of Oldham Street,
ccadilly, on the site previously
ccupied by the Albion Hotel.

n 8 May 1979 the Piccadilly
ore caught fire in the furnishing
epartment on the first floor,
sulting in the death of ten people.
he disaster brought in its wake the
andatory fitting of sprinkler systems
large department stores, codes
the types of material that could

be used as fillings for sofas and easy
chairs, and the requirement for shop
staff to undergo fire training.

Today St. Mary's Gate has lost the
small park across the road from the
Woolworth's store seen in our 1970s
image, and in its place are modern
retail and office buildings.

Spring Gardens Banking History

wealth, prosperity and confidence to its customers.

Today the building is used as a bar and has been renamed The Athenaeum, not to be confused with the other Manchester building bearing this name that was designed by Sir Charles Barry and became known as a prominent lecture hall and library. The bar has retained several architectural features from the building's long banking past including the impressive Ionic marble columns and open space of the main banking hall.

Our picture of the National Westminster Bank at the corner of Spring Gardens and York Street was taken on 15 September 1970.

The building was designed and constructed by Charles Heathcote for Parrs Bank in 1902. Heathcote also designed two other bank buildings in Manchester: the Eagle Star Building on Cross Street in 1911, and Lloyds Bank on King Street in 1915.

Customers entered this Edwardian Baroque building through a mahogany-lined foyer. The banking hall's ceiling was covered with very expensive, very ornate moulded plasterwork and the walls clad in even more expensive green marble. On sunny days the sun's rays, filtered through stained glass windows, created a riot of colour. Unfortunately only a handful of the stained glass windows have survived to the present day. Many of these buildings were lavishly decorated in order to suggest

National Westminster Bank

Edwardian Splendour

Manchester Victoria Station has a history going back over 160 years, and our image taken in the 1970s shows the continued popularity of the station for Manchester commuters.

There is a branch of Lloyd's Bank on the corner, Nellie's fruitier and florist shops and the Silverpool Restaurant, all conveniences ideally placed for commuters who had a little time to spare before their train departed.

The station was designed by George Stephenson and opened in 1844 as a joint station for the Liverpool & Manchester, and the Manchester & Leeds railway companies. Victoria was once linked by a platform to its neighbouring Manchester Exchange Station. The Edwardian Baroque iron and glass frontage was completed as part of the extensions designed by William Dawes and finally completed

n the early 1900s. The façade was threatened in 1996 when the IRA bomb exploded in the city centre causing extensive damage.

Thankfully the façade was renovated and the long glazed canopy still displays the destinations once possible to reach from Victoria when the station was the hub of the Lancashire & Yorkshire Railway Company. While inside the building, near the Edwardian ticket office, there is a tiled map on the wall depicting the Lancashire & Yorkshire region at the height of its network.

The station was also the home of the highly regarded Manchester Victoria signalling school and the large-scale model railway once operated by trainee signallers was considered important enough to be moved to York Railway Museum, where it is occasionally operated for the benefit of visitors.

Though there is little difference between our pictures as regard the external appearance of Victoria, it was heavily remodelled internally in the early 1990s to accommodate Manchester's Metrolink service.

A Chequered Past for this Lost Hotel

The Grosvenor Hotel was listed in the 1890 edition of Baedeker's guide to Great Britain as a commercial hotel where guests could expect to pay around four shillings a night for a room, and half-a-crown or so for dinner.

The Grosvenor offered guests a restaurant, grill room, billiard room, public lounges, ballroom and fifty stockrooms, though its main selling point at one time was 'running water in all 100 bedrooms.

The Grosvenor Hotel was chosen as a venue for many organisations over the years. On the 15 February 1899 a group of 11 operatic and dramatic societies met to discuss the creation of a Mutual Aid Society for the Amateur Theatre. This meeting led to the formation of the National Amateur Operatic and Dramatic Association.

In 1954 the Grosvenor Hotel hosted the British National Science Fiction Convention. The guest of honour that year was John Russell Fearn, a British writer famous in both the UK and the US for writing Westerns, Crime Fiction and pulp Science Fiction. Although Fearn passed away in 1960 his novels and short stories continue to be in print to this day. Fearn wrote under his own name as well as many pseudonyms, perhaps his most prolific being Vargo Statten.

Our picture taken in the early 1970s shows a wet and rainy Deansgate, the Grosvenor Hotel's rooftop signs having faded over the decades. The statue of Oliver Cromwell can be seen to the right of our image. This statue was eventually moved from Deansgate to Wythenshawe Park in the 1980s.

Changing Role for Rochdale Canal

This picture taken in 1971 shows the derelict state of the Rochdale Canal in the vicinity of its junction with the Bridgewater system.

Between 1855 and 1888 the canal was leased to the Lancashire & Yorkshire and other railway companies at an annual fee of around £37,000 a year.

In order to consolidate the business the Rochdale Canal Company brought a large proportion of haulage 'in-house' in 1887 when it put its own fleet of barges into service. As well as cutting operating costs, the company-owned fleet offered greater flexibility and their boats rarely ran empty on their return journeys.

During the Great War, with its best barges requisitioned for service

on the French canal system, the Rochdale Canal Company struggled to maintain its services. Things didn't improve with the Armistice, as the cessation of hostilities saw thousands of former military road vehicles sold off cheaply. The result was a massive increase in the number of road haulage firms competing for canal business, and by mid-1921 the Rochdale Canal Company's freight traffic had fallen so dramatically that the company sold off their remaining fleet to commercial carriers.

There was a period during the Second World War when it looked as though there might be a substantial increase in canal traffic; the government was suggesting the possibility of increased business via canals, and on that basis the Canal Company invested heavily in refurbishing the system. Unfortunately there was no increase in canal traffic and in 1952 the Canal Company applied to Parliament for a Bill to close the navigation. Despite some strong opposition the Bill got through, though the company were obliged to keep the section between Castlefield and Dale Street open as it formed a link between the Manchester & Ashton-under-Lyme, Peak Forest & Macclesfield, and Bridgewater Canal.

Since the 1970s the Rochdale Canal has undergone repairs and the Castlefield and Deansgate areas of the canal have been opened up more to pedestrians. The waterway itself was renovated in 2002 ensuring that the entire canal was once more completely navigable.

Tudor Surprise in the City Centre

Our image shows the flower beds at Ordsall Hall being tended in preparation for the hall's opening to the public, marked by two days of celebrations in April 1972.

The hall is over 800 years old and has had several functions in Manchester's history, including at one time being let to Haworth's Mill to be used as a working men's club.

Most notably Ordsall Hall was the home of the Radclyffe family for over 300 years and during the turbulent years of Tudor England Ordsall was a comparatively safe house for followers of the Catholic religion.

The Radclyffes gave shelter to both Catholic priests and Catholics on the run from the authorities. Among those known to have sheltered here was Robert Catesby who had taken

part in the Earl of Essex's rebellion and was also implicated in a plot to poison Elizabeth I.

Between 1758 and 1959 the hall was owned by the Egertons, after which it passed into the hands of Salford Corporation in 1959. The Council had to undertake some major restoration work before the hall and gardens could be opened to the public.

Today Ordsall Hall is always busy with exhibitions, workshops, family fundays, events and activities for locals and visitors alike. The hall itself retains many of the original beautiful black and white half-timbered Tudor features in its interior.

Manchester's Artistic Past and Future

This image is of Mosley Street, at the corner of Charlotte Street, looking towards St. Peter's Square in August 1972. The Portico Library, opened in 1806 for Manchester businessmen to have a newsroom and library facility, is directly behind our photographer.

Looking down the street the famous Manchester Art Gallery Doric column frontage can be seen.

The gallery was originally constructed by Sir Charles Barry after he won the design competition in 1824. Barry was also responsible for the design of the Houses of Parliament in Westminster. Manchester Art Gallery houses examples of many of the world's greatest artists, including Turner, Rossetti, Gainsborough and Ford Madox Brown. The gallery has over 25,000 works displayed on three floors including oil paintings, watercolours, ceramics, glass, costumes and other decorative art.

The building was extended to incorporate the Athenaeum building, also built by Sir Charles Barry, where much of the collection is also displayed. Originally the Athenaeum, built in 1837, was designed for the use of Manchester's businessmen and elite as a Gentlemen's Club.

However, the Athenaeum is more widely known as a centre for the development of Manchester's cultural, scientific and literary life. There were many famous writers, politicians, scientists and philosophers who gave lectures at the Athenaeum including Charles Dickens, John Ruskin and Disraeli to name a few.

Today Mosley Street is still a vital and bustling thoroughfare with a steady stream of trams, buses and pedestrians at all hours of the day and night. The area has been extensively redeveloped in recent years and many of the old buildings have been renovated revealing the beautiful Victorian and Edwardian façades.

Vibrant Markets

St. Ann's Square at the heart of Manchester's busy shopping district is one of the most vibrant and busy sections of the city and has witnessed several alterations over the centuries.

The square is named after the 18th-century church which stands to the south of the square. Our image taken in May 1973 shows that the area was still open to road traffic and shops lined both sides of the street.

During the Second World War St. Ann's Square underwent a different kind of transformation when sections of the square were used to accommodate air raid shelters that could hold up to 170 people.

The pedestrianisation of St. Ann's Square in 1984 changed the tone of the shopping area and many of the old buildings were altered

internally to accommodate the select boutiques keen to move into the area. Although the interiors changed there are more restrictions on the façades of the buildings as the square is in a conservation area.

Part of the rejuvenation of the square has been the introduction of European and Christmas Markets. Brightly coloured stalls are set up within the square tempting the passersby to sample new food, drinks and purchase unusual gift items. The square has even hosted Manchester's Food and Drink Festival in 2006 and the Jazz Festival in 2007.

Salford's Redeveloped Docklands

This is No.9 Dock in the 1970s taken from the container terminal. The container terminal itself had a quay length of 250 metres (850ft) and was equipped with a pair of Stothert & Pitt container gantry cranes.

Round-the-clock working enabled a 500-capacity container ship to be turned round in just 48 hours.

The vessels featured in our picture are, left to right: the Dubrovnick registered *Korcula*, just arrived from Pyreas; the *Clan Grant* arrived from South Africa and the *Egidia* arrived from Bombay. Also alongside the Clan Grant is the port's 60-ton floating crane.

By the end of the 1970s things were going badly for the upper reaches of the Ship Canal. Competition was forcing ship owners to demand ever faster turn round times in

ports and the extra day it took for a ship to travel up the Canal to discharge or take on cargo in Manchester suddenly became of vital economic importance. The increasing dimensions of new-build container ships and bulk carriers meant that many were too big to navigate the Ship Canal.

These factors together with the changing face of industry and commerce in the North West, including the transfer by Manchester Liners to Ellesmere Port, meant that the end of Salford Docks as a major port was at hand. The docks closed in the early 1980s and work soon

began on reducing its infrastructure to rubble or scrap iron.

For many years the Salford Docks remained silent, until the area was recognised as a perfect place for urban regeneration. Many of the empty warehouses once used for storage were bought by developers who had an idea to transform these old giants into viable and affordable office and living spaces.

Closed Station has a New Purpose

Opened by the Liverpool and Manchester Railway in September 1830, Liverpool Road was the eastern terminus of the first railway in the world to offer a passenger service linking two major cities, and it remained in use as such until superceded by Manchester Victoria in 1844.

For the next 130 years Liverpool Road served as a goods station until it finally closed in 1975 as the need for transporting goods by rail had begun to decrease.

The building at the corner of Liverpool Road and Water Street pre-dated the railway by 13 years but was incorporated into the station and used as the agent's house.

Our image dating from 1979, was in a period of time when the building was

out of use and prior to its restoration as an integral part of the Manchester Museum of Science and Industry.

The old Liverpool Road Station was granted a grade I protected status, and funding provided by the Heritage Lottery Fund and the European Regional Development Fund ensured that the restoration of this important historic building was completed in September 2000.

Joseph Holt Ltd

In the 19th Century beer production in Manchester was lucrative to both the economy and the city's social wellbeing. The government as a whole was able to claim nearly a quarter of its revenues, at the time, from the excise duty levied on beer.

The rise in the number of public houses steadily grew and the people of Manchester enjoyed frequenting them as a place to unwind, especially after a hard day's physical labour in one of the city's many mills or factories.

Raised the son of a weaver in the small textile village of Unsworth, Joseph Holt was attracted to the business opportunities offered by the burgeoning city of Manchester and took his first job as a carter at Harrison's Strangeways Brewery.

Joseph married a schoolteacher with an astute mind for business, and their first brewery in 1849 was a small building behind a pub on Oak Street in the city. By 1855 they had moved to the Ducie Bridge Brewery where Joseph Holt would lend money to publicans in return for 5 per cent interest and the sale of his beer.

In 1860 Joseph Holt had built a brand new brewery, called the Derby Brewery on Empire Street, in Cheetham Hill, pictured below, where the brewery still stands and operates from today.

Despite the deep depression of the early 1860s, due to the Lancashire Cotton Famine brought on by the American Civil War, Joseph Holt bravely changed his strategy. Instead of selling beer at wholesale prices, he decided to open his own managed public houses, selling beer at retail prices.

In 1882 Joseph Holt handed control of the business to his son, Edward Holt, by which time the family company already had 20 public houses to their name. Edward Holt quickly established himself as a successful entrepreneur, and, as did many figureheads within the brewery trade, he turned his hand to local politics. Of greatest significance was his work with the Council to bring soft water to the homes of the people of Manchester from the Lake District, via 70 miles of pipeline, a source that is still used today.

This achievement saw him elected as Lord Mayor of Manchester in 1908, a decision that sparked much controversy with his links to the brewery trade. However, the Manchester public held a different view and he was re-elected for a second term.

For over 150 years, there have been few changes to the original brewing process at the Derby Brewery. The brewery itself has retained its traditional style, although all of the plant has been replaced and expanded over the years, and where necessary modern high-tech equipment is used. The company sources whole cone hops from England along with the best quality English malt, to bring drinkers a choice of beers each with their own unique taste.

The range of bottled and draught beers produced by Joseph Holt can be enjoyed in one of the 132 Joseph Holt's houses in and around

for 40 years. The building was converted into a pub in 1955 and has recently undergone extensive renovation and refurbishment.

Today, the Chief Executive of Joseph Holt is Richard Kershaw, the son of Peter Kershaw, great grandson of the founder. With well-structured schemes in place to ensure Holt's retains control over the brewery process, the good beer speaks for itself in terms of legacy. The bottled beers have been particularly successful in winning prestigious taste awards within the brewery industry and with major UK retailers. As well as being renowned for its beers, Joseph Holt offers a selection of quality food and specially selected wines across its estate of pubs.

A famous name on the streets of Manchester, Joseph Holt was voted one of the city's greatest ever business leaders by *Manchester Evening News* readers.

Joseph Holt has supported local charities since its early beginnings, in particular the Christie Hospital in Manchester, the largest single-site

the Greater Manchester area. The flagship pub is The Woodthorpe, pictured below, another piece of the Joseph Holt heritage. The building was constructed in 1861 and was purchased as a home by Sir Edward Holt Senior in 1888 where he lived

ancer research and treatment centre
n Europe.

n 1914 Sir Edward Holt Senior
elped raise funds to purchase
adium for the Manchester and
District Radium Institute, later named
he Holt Radium Institute in his
onour, which finally amalgamated
vith the Christie Hospital in 1932.

When Sir Edward's son, the second
ir Edward, took over the family
usiness, Holt's support of Christie's
ncreased. When Sir Edward's wife,
ady Margaret died in 1996, she left
Christie's £7 million of her shares in
he brewery.

Joseph Holt brewery has continued
to support Christie's, - even naming
a beer in the hospital's honour. In
1999, during Joseph Holt's 150th
year in business, its customers and
staff raised £301,000 to upgrade the
Outpatients Department at Christie's.
This resulted in the outpatients
entrance being named the Holt
Entrance.

No group or organisation has done
more for Christie's cause, and this
has been achieved largely through
the loyalty and support of all Holt's
customers.

There are few family breweries left
in Britain today; most have been
swallowed up by the giants of the
industry. Holt's is one that has
survived where the emphasis is firmly
placed on great food, as well as a
great pint!

Manchester Rubber Stamp Company Ltd

Manchester Rubber Stamp Company was founded by chemical merchant Walter Edward Hughes in 1880. Their first offices were located on Tib Street in Manchester, as pictured below, where they sold rubber stamps and inks. The traditional process of producing a rubber stamp involved typesetting by hand, using plaster moulds and gas vulcanisers.

The company changed hands in 1920 when Mr A Schofield, a stockbroker, saw the potential in the business and bought it with his business partner Mr H. Radford. With a new management team, the company moved premises to Tower Works on Withy Grove, another part of the city with strong links to the print industry.

The Second World War left deep impressions upon the city, and the lives of the city's residents; the Manchester Rubber Stamp Company and its staff were also affected. Staff numbers reduced as many went to complete their military service. There were shortages of materials and wartime constraints meant that many materials could not even be used. The Tower Works site felt the impact of the Manchester Blitz, and staff upon returning to work discovered that all the windows and doors had been blown out due to bomb blasts.

By the late 1950s the business had expanded and offered engraving as a service. Second premises were acquired at No. 2 Thomas Street, Shudehill, to accomodate the new engraving division. A few years later on 8 April 1963, Geoff A. Hewitt joined the company working at the Shudehill site. By 1970 Geoff was in charge of the entire engraving section of the business and would eventually take over the entire company in 1999.

In 1971 the Manchester Rubber Stamp Company moved to 63 Red Bank where they can still be found today. The engraving side of the business was continuing to expand, so larger premises were needed in order for the company to meet customer demands.

The company's portfolio has come a long way from their humble beginnings as solely a rubber stamp manufacturer. Today the company offers a wide range of products from office signs to memorial boards and plaques. The Manchester Rubber Stamp Company has embraced new technology, using CNC machinery and lasers for manufacturing stamps and engraving. Despite this progress, the business still offers the 'old fashioned' services of yesteryear for its customers.

The company was asked to engrave commemorative plaques for royalty during the Manchester Commonwealth Games. They also produced the electrical tags for the main engineering contractor working at the event.

Still going strong after 120 years, the company serves many blue chip organisations and sources regular work from local authorities as well as the building, electrical and engineering trade.

John Bradshaw and Son Ltd

It was back in 1884 that John Bradshaw & Son Ltd started trading in Heaviley, Stockport.

Originally the firm began trading as coal merchants, as mining was one of the main sources of work during this era Stockport was one of the principle markets in the North West needing coal to power the steam engines in its many textile mills.

After the First World War and into the 1920s the coal industry underwent a period of industrial disputes, with workers striking for better pay and conditions. By 1920 John Bradshaw & Son had made the commercial decision to change their business and become a professional removal and storage service. This transition, that still underpins their core business activities to this very day.

The change in business also heralded a change of location as they moved to new premises at Chestergate in the heart of Stockport.

After the Second World War, removal and storage as an industry, saw significant growth. John Bradshaw & Son was quick to react to this change in fortune.

In the 1970s, Bradshaw's was sold to Blatchpack Ltd of Exeter whose

owner Derek Blatchford became President of the British Association of Removers (B.A.R) in 1980.

Malcolm Halley (the current owner) bought John Bradshaw & Son in 1982 and re-established the 'hub' of the operation back in the North West, and Manchester.

The business moved to Roundthorn Estate, Wythenshawe, in 1990, but the continued growth of the company meant they needed bigger premises. In 2003, it moved to premises on Marshall Stevens Way in Trafford Park, at the site of a former dye works. The premises had actually been built for another removal

firm and when they moved out of the Manchester area Bradshaw's seized the opportunity to acquire the perfectly sized and equipped premises for themselves.

Marshall Stevens Way in Trafford Park is named after the inspirational Marshall Stevens who, along with 69 other men, pioneered the development of the Manchester Ship Canal. Defying all negative criticisms and persevering through many years of obstacles, debates and cash related problems he finally saw the canal open in 1894.

John Bradshaw & Son Ltd, run a successful 24 hour removal business,

known locally as Britannia, whilst conducting business both in the UK and overseas.

They now also trade under the brand of BCL. This division specialises in removals for commercial offices. The Company has partnerships with Manchester City Council, Manchester City Football Club, Co-Operative Group, GMPTE, and all of Manchester's Universities.

From its roots in Stockport, the Company remains close to its trade body, B.A.R, and has been awarded Commercial Remover of the Year twice in the last three years.

Fred Aldous

Founded in 1886 and nestled in the heart of Manchester's city centre is the family owned art, crafts & design materials supplier Fred Aldous. The shop is an Aladdin's cave of paints, pencils, beads, brushes - a kaleidoscope of colour.

Originally the business began with a handcart on Elbow Street supplying canes and willows to make skips and baskets for the cotton trade. By 1902 Fred Aldous I extended the family business to include his son Fred Aldous II.

Although many Manchester companies suffered and declined during the economic depression of the 1920s Fred Aldous was an exception. It was during this time that Fred Aldous II recognised the potential for the family business to develop into supplying arts and crafts materials. It did not take long for this new aspect of the business to gain in popularity and it rapidly became the core of the family business.

Finally in the 1930s Fred Aldous I retired from the business and handed responsibility for the family fortunes onto his son. By 1946, 60 years after the founding of 'Fred Aldous Ltd' the company finally became a private limited company.

e popularity of arts and crafts ntinued into the 1950s and ed Aldous' moved their shop d office areas to a new location Manchester on Withy Grove. the 1960s and the advent of evisions in the home, 'Fred dous Ltd' witnessed a slump in de as more and more people anged how they spent their free ne. A decision was made to sell e Withy Grove shop and move e family business temporarily to Back Piccadilly, before finally tling into 37 Lever Street where e company still trades.

1970 Christopher Fred Aldous III came Managing Director, taking

over from Fred Aldous II who after 68 years became Chairman of the business, taking a back seat in the day to day running of the shop. By 1978 'Fred Aldous Ltd' expanded further by buying a manufacturing building in Peak Dale in order to create many of their products themselves.

As with many other businesses in Manchester, the introduction of a computer was revolutionary, and in 1987 'Fred Aldous Ltd' integrated their first computer into the invoicing process. Until this point every invoice the company produced was still typed on an old

typewriter. Today the shop has its own website, blog and even ebay site in order to promote the company and ease the manner in which customers can purchase their goods from a selection of over 25,000 products.

Since 1886 many of the Aldous family have taken instrumental roles within the company. Under their guidance 'Fred Aldous Ltd' has remained one of Manchester's leading providers of art, crafts and design material.

Professional Footballers Association

The first meeting of the PFA took place in Manchester's Imperial Hotel in December 1907 under the leadership of the Manchester United and Wales winger, Billy Meredith. Meredith and many of his football colleagues were discussing the all important questions of the day: better pay and the problems with transfer restraints.

At the time the retain and transfer system meant that even though a players contract with the club had expired the player himself could not play for anyone else or arrange another contract until the club sanctioned his transfer.

The efforts of Billy Meredith and the support of the newly formed union were instrumental in making changes to the Factory Acts, which in turn allowed the ordinary working man Saturday afternoons off. By 1909 the newly formed union was on the brink of strike, and eventually settled for recognition of its status as a union and the opportunity of top-ups to the players' weekly salary with bonus payments.

As with so many families and communities the First World War left its mark and the PFA was no exception to this. On July 1 1916 Evelyn Lintott, PFA chairman, England International and player for Bradford and QPR, was killed during action on the Somme as he led a platoon of men over the top.

Perhaps one of the PFA's most influential chairmen and one of Manchester United's more celebrated captains, Charlie Roberts, took the union to new heights in 1919. He ensured that player's wages gained an unprecedented level of £9 per week, almost double what they had previously been on.

During the 1920s Britain underwent a huge depression which left very few families unaffected. Money was tight and jobs were few and far between. This was also a lean time for the PFA, who saw their membership suffer.

It was while the union was under the guidance of Jimmy Fay, also affectionately known as 'Gentlemen Jim', that the crucial Henry Leddy case came to court. This case proved that the law could not allow the arbitrary breaking of agreements between players and their clubs, Leagues or Associations.

In his time as the union secretary in the 1950s Jimmy Hill was instrumental in the forging of the current name of the union to the Professional Footballer's Association. The 1960s heralded a crucial development in football as under the direction of a new chairman, Jimmy Hill, the PFA ensured that the maximum wage restriction for players was abolished.

Over the decades the PFA has also been at the forefront of creating funds for the support of players including the Provident Fund, the Accident Fund, the Benevolent Fund and the Education Fund.

Gordon Taylor, ex-player for Bolton Wanderers, Birmingham City and Blackburn Rovers, became Chief Executive of the PFA in 1981, and under his guidance the PFA continues its development of community programmes. The union moved into new offices in Manchester; the Players' Cash Benefit Scheme was put in place and a new standard contract and non-contributory pension scheme was implemented.

Today the PFA's links with Manchester are still going strong. As part of their 100th year celebrations the union has launched the "One Goal One Million" campaign. They aim to raise £1 million to fund the new development of the Children's Rehabilitation and Physiotherapy Unit at the University Children's Hospital, Manchester.

HMG Paints

Back in 1930 Harold Marcel Guest, a former travelling salesman, started a business in his own name, H. Marcel Guest Paints (HMG Paints). Producing cellulose capping solutions for medicinal bottle tops, Guest employed three other members of staff: Herbert Falder the grandfather of the current Managing Director, Stanley Wallwork and Bertram Bernie.

An accident led to the discovery of cellulose paint when some capping solvent was carelessly thrown and stripped the paint from Marcel Guest's car. An improvised coating was quickly formulated to conceal the damage and it proved to be a winning formula. However Marcel Guest felt that paint was not his forté, so Herbert Falder paid £100 to buy him out, including the rights to the company name.

After three years the entire company moved to Fitzgeorge Street in the Irk Valley on a single horse and cart. Here they remained until 1959 when they moved to their current riverside site in Collyhurst, along the banks of Manchester's lost river, the River Irk. This was a prime location for manufacturing as just up the river was one of Manchester's first water-driven cotton mills.

Herbert's son, Brian Falder joined the business full time in 1945 and ran the company for 40 years overseeing an overwhelming period of growth before semi-retiring as Chairman in the 1990s. Brian then handed the reins to his sons, John and Stephen, who are now Managing Director and Marketing Director respectively.

The Falders are not the only family to work in the business; throughout the years there has been a strong tradition of local families working alongside one another at Collyhurst Road. A true HMG legend is 82 year old Albert Moore who started with HMG in 1933 delivering paint with a bicycle and sidecar, and continued working part time for the company when most other employees would have retired.

Remaining true to their community and heritage, HMG have helped to transform their surroundings over the last 50 years to an environmentally conscious, green, woodland delight, thanks to their tree planting campaign. Given the name the New Era Woods after the original HMG factory, the woods are now used as an invaluable educational resource for local schools.

Today HMG employs around 165 dedicated staff at its Collyhurst headquarters. They have a network of subsidiary and associate companies across Europe, America and the Middle East, and produce millions of litres of paint every year. Including thousands of types of applications, such as wood coatings for furniture, special coatings for light bulbs and grass paints for sports stadia. HMG Paints can be found on every continent and on virtually every material from steel and glass to concrete and grass.

Rhenus Hauser Limited

With a turnover in excess of £33 million, 9 strategically placed offices throughout England and Scotland, and a reputation for being a major international freight specialist; it is hard to believe that Rhenus Hauser Limited began in the modest surroundings of Paul Hauser's Timperley home.

Born in Switzerland in 1895 Paul Hauser became a football player for FC Basle and later transferred to FC Zurich. It was during this time that he also completed his International Transport Apprenticeship. Eventually moving to Manchester, he founded P Hauser & Co taking full advantage of the excellent transport links that the city offers.

During the Second World War, Navy convoys ensured that P Hauser & Co were able to continue to run their freight service through the docks at Liverpool. However, it wasn't until after the war in 1946 that Hauser developed their direct rail service. This service meant that they could offer clients the opportunity to send their goods from Manchester to the continent in approximately 10 days.

In the 1950s Hauser recognised the developing Manchester rail network as an opportunity to solidify

the company's transport base by acquiring its own rail depot at Ardwick East Goods Station; he also changed the company name to P Hauser Ltd.

In the 1960s and 1970s the company expanded into road trailer operations and also developed a close relationship with air services by opening a new office at Stansted airport. These new developments meant that P Hauser Ltd retained its position at the forefront of sea, air, rail and road freight services.

Today Rhenus Hauser Limited has over 70 years of proven expertise and delivers around 200,000 consignments every year to over 20 European countries. Although the company has expanded to include offices in Basildon, Bradford, Bristol, Cannock, Glasgow, Hull, Leighton Buzzard, Newton Aycliffe and Sheffield, the head-office is still in Manchester at Trafford Park. Throughout the company's sustained growth and success over the years, they have retained their strong links with Manchester and continue to be one of the UK's leading providers of freight logistic solutions.

Lancashire Eccles Cakes Limited

It was over 80 years ago that Samuel Edmonds began supplying Manchester's grocers with a range of bread and confectionary. Distribution started with horsedrawn vans, but with the advent of the motorcar they were replaced by model T Fords.

After several years the business expanded and Samuel was joined by his sons Samuel Jnr, Stanley and Leonard, and in 1938 Edmonds Bakeries Limited was formed. From these newly opened premises on Hyde Road in West Gorton the family was able to manufacture a larger range of confectionary and further expand their distribution. They became suppliers to Belle Vue amusement park and local agencies.

Due to the expansion of the supermarkets in the early 1960s and the demise of local grocers, the pattern of trade changed and the family decided that specialisation was the way forward.

The company's name was changed to Edmonds Eccles Cakes Limited and became the largest producer of Eccles Cakes in the country. In fact, the bakery was so successful that after several years it was acquired by Park Cake Bakeries, Oldham. Despite the change in ownership the company continued to be run successfully by Ken, the youngest member of the family. After the acquisition of Park Cake Bakeries, by Northern Foods, Ken resigned and in 1978 formed a new family business Lancashire Eccles Cakes Limited. The modern purpose build bakery is located on Hyde Road in Ardwick and using the original family recipe produces Eccles Cakes, still made in the traditional method - by hand.

The business is still an independent family-run concern. Ken's daughter and Managing Director, Ann, says, "although our bakery is very modern we are true to my father's concept that we should make our cakes just like you would at home – but on a much bigger scale. All our cakes are handmade." Ann's brother and Production Director, Ian, explains, "we only use the very best ingredients."

Their Eccles Cakes are packed with Vostizza A currants surrounded by melt in the mouth puff pastry. The currants are the best money can buy from a Greek farmers' co-operative in the ancient town of Aeghion (formerly Vostizza), near to Corinth, from whose name we get the word currant. Many tons of currants and raisins are used each week.

Despite being ready washed, on arrival at the bakery the dried fruit is washed again allowing it to plump up ready for baking. Mixed with butter and sugar, the currants make up the filling of the cakes. The puff pastry that envelopes the mouth-watering fruit is made from untreated flour and top quality dairy butter. "The ingredients are the key to our cakes," explains Ian. "Great quality ingredients simply put together".

Today, as the trend for traditional, wholesome products increases Real Lancashire Eccles Cakes have proved to be even more popular with the general public, and can be found in top supermarkets, delicatessens and local corner shops. These Lancashire delicacies are exported to Europe and the USA. You may even spot them on the shelves of shops abroad when on holiday – reminding you of that taste of home!

So after many decades the Edmonds family are still producing the finest Eccles Cakes. Have they changed? Not at all. They still have the same buttery taste - Real Lancashire, Real Eccles Cakes, and Real Good!

Manchester Businesses

Wilson Gunn

John G Wilson opened his first office on Market Street in 1864. Manchester by this time had established itself as the first industrial city of the Industrial Revolution and business was in full flow.

Wilson Gunn had a prime location in Manchester and, with so many of the emerging industrialists requiring their inventions to be patented, the company had a continuous source of work.

Over one hundred years later in the 1970s, the company moved to new offices in the Royal Exchange Building. The Royal Exchange is still one of Manchester's strongest visual links to the city's industrial past. This grand Victorian building once held one of the largest cotton trading rooms in Britain until 1968 when trading was drawn to a close. In 1976 it changed usage once more and became home to the Royal Exchange Theatre group. Unfortunately the building suffered devastating consequences because of the Manchester bomb in 1996 with extensive damage that left tenants of the building waiting two years for repairs to be completed.

The company, now known as Wilson Gunn, moved offices to Blackfriars House, the refined 1926 building that borders the River Irwell. The building was built by Harry Fairhurst for the Bleachers Association, a union of 53 companies who were involved in the bleaching and finishing of any cotton materials.

Although Wilson Gunn has offices in other major cities throughout the UK, their roots remain firmly in the city of Manchester. The company continues to grow from strength to strength, and now services clients from all leading industry sectors. As Wilson Gunn can testify, innovation has and always will flourish in the city of Manchester.

REWCO

essential to the industrial development of Manchester and in 1930 Rochdale had an abundance of mills and factories for engineering and textile production.

In an ideal location, the business provided maintenance services to the industrial steam market. William Ranson also manufactured his own welding rods; they were something you simply could not buy at that time.

Since the company started, the business has passed through three generations of the Ingoe family and is today managed by John Ingoe, who took over the company in 1983. With a factory based at Queensway in Rochdale, the company runs its

administration from converted offices at Dingle Farm in Middleton.

Today, Rochdale Electric Welding Company provides boiler repairs and installation services around the clock, as well as continuing their services to the ever-changing steam market.

Rochdale Electric Welding Company formed when William Ranson Ingoe moved from South Shields in Tyneside, where the closure of shipyards had dried up local work. He saw the potential of business in Manchester, a city that was thriving through industry, and started Rochdale Electric Welding Company in 1930 from a factory in Rochdale. Steam power has always been

Laurence Supply Company Ltd

Handbags have always been a desired fashion accessory and at no other time could they be more sought after than in the 1960s. Casper Gordon, the founder of Laurence Supply Company Ltd recognised the potential and started his own business designing and manufacturing handbags.

Casper Gordon originally worked as a raincoat cutter before the advent of the Second World War. As many other young men did, Gordon signed up and joined the Desert Rats, fighting in the Middle East against Rommel's troops in the Western Desert. In 1943 under enemy fire, he was shot and badly injured. He found himself hospitalised in Cairo where he spent his recuperation period learning to make handbags; a form of therapy which the hospital staff encouraged. Upon his return to Britain, Casper soon came to learn that his former job had gone and so he decided to make use of his new found skills and started his own handbag business.

By 1965 Laurence Supply Company was an established handbag manufacturer, based at a factory on Regent Road. At the time Regent Road was a hustle-bustle location, full of shops and markets.

She's a **MACKESON** type

...and all the better for it !

For the next ten years the firm produced handbags and in 1973 became a limited company. Not long after, in 1977, it became apparent that it was no longer economical to continue making handbags in Manchester.

Laurence Supply therefore turned their attentions to importing and exporting handbags, along with purses, wallets and belts. The business was handed down to Casper Gordon's son, Laurence, and new premises were sought at Midland Street in Ardwick. Today they operate with a team of 12 experienced staff including Laurence's son, Mark, sourcing the latest styles of handbags direct from catwalks across the world.

Now the Laurence Supply team attend key fashion events around the world for inspiration for new designs. Ensuring that their well-known UK high-street clients have their own unique collections each season. They now have a warehouse and administration centre in Luton and their own haulage fleet, which means they can offer quick deliveries to clients.

Although the manufacturing process has moved to the Far East, Laurence Supply remain instrumental in the design of their handbags. A short trip to the factory floor to check manufacture is no longer an option, however Laurence Supply are soon to establish a permanent CCTV link to their Hong Kong counterparts allowing them to clutch as tight a hold of the manufacturing reigns as possible.

KE Cars

Wythenshawe Hall and parklands were given to Manchester as an open space in 1926. Later Wythenshawe was to become a garden city and have one of the largest council estates in the Manchester area.

Kenneth Emery, from Wythenshawe, first started to drive taxis with a friend in 1958 as a sideline job. Business continued to grow, but complications arose when the Council threatened to evict Kenneth Emery from his council house for running two cars from the same address.

Ken was a popular face in Wythenshawe, and in July 1969 the news of his eviction hit the headlines in the *Wythenshawe Express & Recorder*. The majority of Wythenshawe, including his local customers, rallied to support him.

The eviction notice was withdrawn upon an official business premises being found, and by 1971 KE Cars were running a full time taxi and wedding car service.

The first wedding car in the company's fleet was a black Humber. Humber cars were renowned for their solid build quality and immaculate interiors, making them perfect for official appointments. The company also had some Ford Zephyrs, and a white Rolls-Royce has been added to the collection in the last twenty years, especially for weddings.

KE Cars have many corporate contracts including the BBC, and many a celebrity has enjoyed one of their luxury vehicles. Kenneth Emery was the chauffeur for the late Bob Monkhouse for nearly 5 years, bringing him to Manchester and escorting him to some of his favourite clubs in Patricroft and Salford.

KE Cars are still located at the garages behind the Portway shops in Wythenshawe. Working together with his daughter, Pauline, it will soon be occasion for KE Cars to celebrate 50 years of service.

Glosta Engineering

The early history of Glosta Engineering dates back to 1973 when the company was first established by Gloria and Stanley Moore. They started as a general engineering and fabrication company at premises on Wellington Street, Bury. Bury was once one of the chief paper making centres in Europe, with its many paper mills.

The company then moved to Kay Brow in Ramsbottom, another town whose existence was enriched by industrialisation with the many textile mills and bleaching factories.

In 1996, Glosta Engineering moved to Bealey Industrial Estate on Dumers Lane in Bury, where they are still located today. The industrial estate is named in memory of the Bealey family, who came to settle in the area back in the late 18th Century, thanks to a bleaching works they owned by the river Irwell.

Glosta Engineering has retained its familial connections, not only does the name Glosta derive from the amalgamation of Gloria and Stanley's names, but their son Gary Moore took over at the helm of the company in 1991, assisted by his sister Samantha.

With the re-development of many parts of the city, there is always substantial demand for skips. Glosta Engineering are an engineering company first and foremost, but they have expertise in designing and manufacturing skips for various trades. The skips are safe and compatible to use with specialist skip loading equipment.

MGP (Employee Benefits) Ltd

The old bank building on the corner of Every Street and Ashton New Road in Ancoats was originally built for the District Bank in the late 19th Century.

The District Bank was formed when the Manchester & Liverpool District Banking Company opened for business in the early 1830s. The bank made numerous acquisitions to achieve growth, and by 1942 had over 130 branches.

Although always known to the public as the District Bank, they were not officially granted this name until 1924.

At the end of the 1960s National Provincial acquired the bank, where it remained as an independent subsidiary until it formed part of the merger that produced the National Westminster Bank in 1970.

The branch closed in the 1970s and in the last ten years the building has been home to MGP Ltd. The company has made substantial improvements to the Bank, both inside and out, restoring the building from its former redundant state. Established in 1974, MGP are independent financial advisors and pension consultants to the corporate market.

As well as assisting businesses with financial employee benefits, such as pensions and private health insurances, MGP has ensured the old bank building is preserved to its original financial origins.

Tuckers Solicitors

Manchester's industrial past is still evident in many of the buildings and streets of the city. By the 1800s inventions such as James Watts rotary steam-engine meant that factories could be built throughout the city rather than on the river. The industrial heart of the city was beginning to change and the population of Manchester had reached an unprecedented 95,000 people.

Workers housing could be found scattered throughout the city either close to the factories or confined to areas like New Cross and Newtown. While workers needed to be close to their workplace, factory owners also wanted to be close to their source of income.

The Mosley Street area, as featured here, offered housing of a different style. Mosley Street became one of the main streets rich factory owners sought for housing to accommodate their needs.

Today Mosley Street is part of Manchester's commercial bustle and businesses like Tuckers Solicitors have established themselves here in the heart of the city.

Founded in 1980 by owner Barry Tucker, criminal defence lawyers Tuckers Solicitors have had strong links with Manchester. They moved offices in the city, until finally settling on Mosley Street.

During the Strangeways Prison riots of 1990 Tuckers Solicitors were instrumental in representing a number of the defendants. Today the Manchester office is run by senior partner Franklin Sinclair and employs 65 members of staff. The company has expanded to include offices in London and Birmingham, making Tuckers Solicitors one of the largest criminal defence law firms in the country.

Compressor Engineering Norwest Ltd

With many factory closures in the Trafford Park area in the 1960s, a local economical decline started and the area slowly become sparse and void of its once thriving business activities.

By 1982 the Salford Docks were officially closed, and at around the same time, the local Salford and Trafford Councils had attempted to bring business back to the area by setting up an enterprise zone initiative.

This initiative encouraged prospects for development by offering businesses exemption from development rates and land tax, as well as simplified planning regulations. Between 1981 and 1985, approximately 300 new businesses started in the Salford Enterprise Zone.

Compressor Engineering Norwest Ltd was one such business. Formed in 1983 the same year that Salford City Council purchased the majority of the docks from the Manchester Ship Canal Company. They were one of the first companies to take residence in the newly developed Salford Quay at Sovereign Enterprise Park.

Compressed air has been used in engineering for many decades, especially for mining and the fabrication of metals. The force generated from compressed air is used to operate numerous tools and instruments. In the 20th Century there has been an increase in the use of compressed air devices as it is non-hazardous, harmless to the environment and can be easily stored and transported.

As service engineers, Compressor Engineering are involved in the servicing and maintenance of compressed air systems. Their team are fully qualified to deliver expert advice to their customers.

Compressor Engineering has worked hard in recent years to promote the use of clean compressed air in the dentistry profession. As well as offering their expert advice, they also conduct full supply, service and support to the profession for compression equipment used, ensuring that all health and safety guidelines are met.

Today the company continues to provide their everyday services with an additional focus on the dental profession, and the use of compressed air driven equipment required for delivering the simplest of everyday dental practices.

Mayfield Storage and Distribution

With the massive urban regeneration and an ever changing skyline, Manchester continues to evolve. There has always been the need for businesses in the area to be able to store consumables in bulk, ready for either use, or transportation throughout the region and further afield.

Mayfield Storage & Distribution is appropriately named after the location where they first started their business, and where they can still be found today, the old Mayfield Railway Station on Fairfield Street.

Mayfield Railway Station first opened to passengers in 1911 as an overspill for the then Manchester London Road Station, which we all know today as Manchester Piccadilly Station. At that time London Road was the gateway to the North West and could not cope with the huge volume of passengers. The Bournemouth to Manchester train, The Pines Express was a popular service from the station. The station finally closed in 1960 due to the decline in the number of passengers and the building was used as a parcel depot from 1970 until 1980.

Father and son team, Alan and Paul Taylor, formed Mayfield Storage & Distribution in 1984. Alan had previously been in the motor trade at Knott Mill, and joined forces with his son, who at the time, was working for British Aerospace at Woodford.

When they first started, approximately 90 per cent of the business involved storing and transporting cotton based raw materials; an appropriate juxtaposition with Manchester's prior rich cotton trade heritage.

With the regeneration of the city, and the continuing growth in construction projects locally, their main business is now the storage and distribution of pre-fabricated buildings. Most buildings today are manufactured overseas due to costs being cheaper on the continent. The buildings are then shipped to the UK as finished goods, where companies like Mayfield Storage & Distribution break them down, store them, and deliver them to the relevant construction sites as and when they are needed.

Many of Manchester's most famous modern buildings including the Beatham Tower and the Royal Bank of Scotland building on Deansgate have been delivered to Manchester via Mayfield Storage & Distribution. Today they store everything from building materials to fancy goods.

Straight Freight (Manchester) Ltd

Trafford Park was the industrial hub of Manchester's engineering and heavy industry business.

With a rich industrial history, Trafford Park's Westinghouse Road is named after British Westinghouse Electric & Manufacturing Company. British Westinghouse was a stalwart in the Trafford Park industrial estate, they built their first factory in 1899, and used American production methods to manufacture turbines and generators.

In 1919 the company became Metropolitan Vickers and in 1959 Associated Electrical Industry (AEI),

until in 1967 (GEC) took over AEI and became one of the biggest employers on the industrial estate for several decades.

Straight Freight (Manchester) Ltd started on Westinghouse Road in 1985, on part of GEC's former site. The company chose Trafford Park due to its excellent motorway links and started running daily services from the UK to Holland and Belgium as an unaccompanied freight forwarder. They finally moved and got their own premises on Textilose Road in Trafford Park.

Assisting with the smooth flow of international trade, Straight Freight has always tailored their services to suit their clients. Requirements have changed in recent times, and no two operations are the same. Such varied needs see the company ship either one full load for one customer, or arrange multiple cargoes to be grouped together and shipped from different sources.

Since the business started, the company now runs daily self-drive trailers throughout mainland Europe, stretching out to Scandinavia and Eastern Europe. Straight Freight have developed their own full, and less than full, container airfreight services, enabling them to import or export to clients anywhere in the world. Today, the haulage and freight industry now sees more trailers carrying more weight and longer working hours for those involved.

Over the last twenty years, Straight Freight have increased the number of trailers they ship per week. They are responsible for various cargoes from chemicals to textiles; through services by land, sea or air. They have won many prestigious awards for the level and type of service they provide.

With more and more freight companies emerging, it is clear that this industry is incredibly competitive. In 1985 it was somewhat different, next day deliveries were rare but today they are commonplace; and rates were very good, but today business can be 'cut throat'.

Owner, Steve Kennedy has a team of skilled staff, benefiting from some of those being multi-lingual as the company looks towards further expansion to new territories in Europe and the Far East.

Bluebird Bus

You would need to travel back to 1824 for the first record of organised transport in Manchester. John Greenwood, owner of the Pendleton toll gates started a regular horse bus service, taking passengers to Manchester's Market Street and allowing them to disembark at anyplace along the route.

Running only three times daily, the vehicles could carry no more than nine passengers, but they became very popular.

John Greenwood Junior took over his father's legacy and in 1865 was pivotal in the formation of a new consortium, the Manchester Carriage Company. Meanwhile larger horse buses were used that could hold up to 40 passengers, taking people through the main roads of the city centre as well as the surrounding districts.

Over a century later, the British Government introduced the 1985 Transport Act and the deregulation of buses outside London. At the time Mike Dunstan was a bus driver at the Princess Road depot for Greater Manchester Buses, and it was this new passing law that gave him the inspiration to provide a service to the public in his local area.

Bluebird Bus & Coach formed in July 1988, having been purchased by members of the Dunstan family. The company first operated from a unit on British Aerospace land, now unrecognisable after extensive redevelopment. In 1994 they moved to their current premises in Middleton, and are one of only a few independent bus operators in Manchester.

Bluebird pioneered the introduction of buses with a low floor design, in the mid 1990s, before legislation was brought in to convert routes to low floor easily accessible buses. The bright blue of the Bluebird buses are a regular sight in the city centre and North Manchester districts. The company today employs 95 staff members, has a fleet of 47 vehicles and buys new vehicles each year.